THE KOREAN WORKERS' PARTY

HISTORIES OF RULING COMMUNIST PARTIES

Richard F. Staar, editor

Korean Workers' Party: A Short History, Chong-Sik Lee

History of Vietnamese Communism, 1925–1976, Douglas Pike

Lenin's Legacy: The Story of the CPSU, Robert G. Wesson

THE KOREAN WORKERS' PARTY: A Short History

CHONG-SIK LEE

HOOVER INSTITUTION PRESS
Stanford University • Stanford, California

The Hoover Institution on War, Revolution and Peace, founded at Stanford University in 1919 by the late President Herbert Hoover, is an interdisciplinary research center for advanced study on domestic and international affairs in the twentieth century. The views expressed in its publications are entirely those of the authors and do not necessarily reflect the views of the staff, officers, or Board of Overseers of the Hoover Institution.

Hoover Institution Publication 185

International Standard Book Number: 0-8179-6852-1
Library of Congress Catalog Card Number: 77-2427
Printed in the United States of America

To
Myung-Sook

Contents

PARTY STRUCTURE OF THE DEMOCRATIC PEOPLES REPUBLIC OF KOREA

Party Congress

(Fifth Congress of the Korean Worker's Party held November 1970. Scheduled to meet every four years)

Inspection (Control) Committee

Chairman
*So Chol

Central Auditing Committee

Chairman
Kim Se-hwal

Central Committee
Secretariat

(in rank order by analytical judgement)

General Secretary
*Kim Il-song

Secretaries

*Kim Il
*Kim Tong-kyu
*O Chin-u
*Yim Chun-chu
*Yon Hyong-muk
*Yang Hyong-sop
*Han Ik-su
*Hyon Mu-kwang
*Kim Yong-nam
*(Kim Chong-il)

Full Members

†An Sung-hak
†Chang Yun-pil
†Chi Pyong-hak
†Choe Chae-u
†Choe Chang-hwan
†Choe Chang-kwon
*Choe Hyon
†Choe In-tok
†Choe Yong-chin
†Choe Yong-im
†Choe Yun-su
†Chon Chae-pong
†Chon Chang-chol
*Chon Mun-sop
†Chon Mun-uk
†Chon Yong-hui
*Chong Chun-ki
†Chong Kyong-hui
†Chong Song-nam
†Chong Tong-chol
†Chong Tong-ik
†Chu To-il
*Han Ik-su
†Ho Tam
†Hong Si-hak
*Hyon Mu-kwang
†Hyon Chol-kyu
†Kim Hoe-il
†Kim Hwan
†Kim Hyok-chol
†Kim I-hun
*Kim Il
†Kim Ik-hyon
*Kim Il-song
†Kim Kuk-hun
†Kim Kuk-tae
†Kim Kwan-sop
†Kim Kye-hyon
†Kim Kyong-yon
†Kim Man-kum
†Kim Nak-hui
†Kim Pyong-ha
†Kim Pyong-yul
†Kim Si-hak
†Kim Sok-hwan
†Kim Sok-ki
†Kim Song-ae
†Kim Su-tuk
†Kim Tae-hong
*Kim Tong-kyu
†Kim Yo-chung
†Kim Yong-chu
*Kim Yong-nam
†Kim Yun-son
†Paek Hak-im
†Pak Hae-kwon
†Pak Mun-kyu
*Pak Song-chol
†Pak Yong-sok
†Pak Yong-sun
†Pak Su-tong
†Pang Hak-se
†Pi Chang-in
†Sin Kyong-chol
*So Chol
†So Kwan-hui
†Song Pok-ki
†Tae Pyong-yol
*Yang Hyong-sop
†Yang Kun-ok
†Yang Man-chol
†Yi Chang-son
†Yi Chi-chan
†Yi Kil-song
†Yi Kon-il
*Yi Kun-mo
†Yi Min-su
†Yi Pyon-sang
†Yi Son-hwa
†Yi Tong-chum
†Yi Tu-ik

Candidate Members

†An Myong-chol
†Chang Chol
†Chang Chong-hwan
†Cho Myong-son
†Choe Chin-son
†Choe Chong-kon
†Chon Ha-chol
†Chon Pyong-ho
†Chon Se-pong
†Chong Chae-kil
†Chu Chang-pok
†Chu Kyu-chang
†Ho Chang-suk
†Ho Yon-suk
†Hyon Chang-yong
†Hyon Chun-kuk
†Im Hyong-ku
†Kang Sok-sung
†Kim Chae-yong
†Kim Chang-pok
†Kim Hong-kwan
†Kim Hyong-ku
†Kim Hyong-pong
†Kim Ki-nam
†Kim Ki-son
†Kim Kum-ok
†Kim Kwang-kuk
†Kim Ui-sun
†Kim Ung-sam
†Kim Yong-yon
†Kye Hyong-sun
†O Kyong-hun
†O Yong-pang
†Paek Pom-su
†Paek Son-Il
†Pak Chun-sik
†Pak Chung-kuk
†Pak Ki-so
†Pak Son-kyun
†Pak Yong-sin
†Sim Chang-wan
†Sin Chin-sun
†So Chang-nam
†So Yun-sok
†Son Kyung-chun
†Son Song-pil
†Wang-Ok-hwan
†Yang Chung-kyom
†Yi Chang-su
†Yi Chol-pong
†Yi Chong-il
†Yi Hong-kyun
†Yi Im-su
†Yi Pil-song

Political Committee

*Kim Il-song
*Kim Il
*Pak Song-chol
*Kim Tong-kyu
*Choe Hyon
*O Chin-u
*So Chol
*Yim Chun-chu
*Yi Kun-mo
*Yon Hyong-muk
*Yang Hyong-sop
*O Paek-yong
*Han Ik-su
*Yi Yong-mu
*Chon Mun-sop
*Yi Chong-ok

Candidate Members

*(Kim Chong-Il)
*Hyon Mu-kwang
*Kim Yong-nam
*Chong Chun-ki
*Kim Chol-man
*Kang Song-san

Since the 1970 Party Congress, North Korea has not announced the membership of the Political Committee. It is ranked above according to analytical judgement.

†Hwang Chang-yop
†Hwang Sun-hui
†Im Chol
†Im Su-man
†Kang Hui-won
†Kang Hyon-su
*Kang Song-san
†Kim Chang-kwon
*Kim Chol-man
*Kim Chong-il
†Kim Chong-yong
†Kim Chung-nin
†Kim Chwa-hyok

†Kong Chin-tae
†Kye Ung-tae
†No Pyong-u
†No Tae-sok
†O Chae-won
*O Chin-u
†O Kul-yol
*O Paek-yong
†O Suk-hui
†O Tae-pong
†O Tong-uk
†Pae Sung-hyok
†Paek Nam-un

†Yi Ul-sol
†Yi Yong-ik
*Yi Yong-mu
†Yi Yong-pok
*Yim Chun-chu
†Yom Tae-chun
*Yon Hyong-muk
†Yu Chang-sik
†Yu Chong-suk
†Yu Sun-hui
†Yu Sung-nam
†Yun Ki-pok

†Kim Nung-il
†Kim Pyong-sam
†Kim Song-kol
†Kim Song-kuk

†Yi Pong-kyom
†Yi Pong-sop
†Yi Pong-won
†Yi Si-won

New members added since 1970
(Deceased members have been dropped.)

Liaison Bureau (South Korean General Bureau)

Central Committee Departments

Administrative
Yi Yong-ho

Agriculture
†Yi Kon-il

Communications

Construction and Transportation
†Pak Yong-sok

Culture and the Arts

Documents (Archives)

External Affairs

Fiscal Planning
†Kim Ung-sam

Fisheries
Yi Sun-kun

Heavy Industry
†Kim Hwan

International
*Kim Yong-nam

Light Industry and Commerce
†Chon Pyong-ho

Military Affairs
†Tae Pyong-yol

Organization and Guidance

Propaganda and Agitation

Science and Education
†Yun Ki-pok

Youth and Juvenile Work
†Chong Chae-kil

Military Committee

Chairman
*Kim Il-song

Provincial Party Committees
and Responsible Secretaries

Chagang
Yi Pong-kil

North Hamgyong
Kim Chi-ku

South Hamgyong
†Yi Kil-song

North Hwanghae
Choe Mun-son

South Hwanghae
Kim Won-chon

Kangwon
†Hong Si-hak

North Pyongan
†Kim Pyong-yul

South Pyongan
†Chong Tong-ik

Yanggang
Yim Su-man

Municipal Party Committees
and Responsible Secretaries

Hamhung City
Hwang Tae-ho

Kaesong City
Chang In-sok

Nampo City
Kim Se-wan

Pyongyang City
†Kang Hyon-su

Sinjuiju City
Paek Si-un

Wonson City
Paek Chong-won

April 1977
U.S. Government Document CR 77-11706

***Political Committee Members**
†Central Committee Members

Editor's Foreword

Chong-Sik Lee's book, *The Korean Workers' Party: A Short History*, is the first in a series of monographs on the histories of the sixteen ruling communist parties from their organization to the present time. The studies were initiated to fill an important gap in modern English-language historiography on communism in Albania, Bulgaria, Cambodia, China, Cuba, Czechoslovakia, (East) Germany, Hungary, (North) Korea, Laos, Mongolia, Poland, Romania, the Soviet Union, Vietnam, and Yugoslavia.

Each volume in the series covers many, if not all, of the following aspects in the specific communist party's history:

- Circumstances of founding, early leading personnel, social composition of membership, initial impact on domestic political life;
- Inter-war party situation emphasizing relations with the Comintern (interference in internal party affairs, participation of party cadres in different Comintern schools, purges of these cadres at home and in the Soviet Union);
- Positions taken and activities during World War II (attitude during the Stalin-Hitler pact, resistance movement and cooperation with other groups, relations toward Moscow before and after Comintern dissolution);
- Stages on the road to power (changes in leadership and composition of membership, electoral participation and results, methods of settling accounts with political allies and adversaries);
- Stalinist phase and purges after World War II;
- Aspects of de-Stalinization and its impact on party relations with the CPSU, and the same in domestic political and socioeconomic affairs;

- Party problems in the late 1970s, with a final overview of the historical role played by the communist party, its functions in domestic politics (revolutionary transformation of the country) and in the multi-faceted relations with the CPSU.

As general editor of the series, I am pleased that such a distinguished scholar as Dr. Chong-Sik Lee accepted our invitation to prepare this history of the communist movement in Korea.

Richard F. Staar
Coordinator of International Studies

Hoover Institution
Stanford University

Preface

When I was asked by the Hoover Institution to write a short history of the Korean Communist movement as a part of its monograph series on world communism, I hesitated to accept the invitation. The question that immediately entered my mind was "What could I add to what has already been published?" Was not our recent work on *Communism in Korea,* coauthored by Professor Robert A. Scalapino and myself and published in early 1973, long enough? Did not that work, and the previous book on the *Korean Communist Movement, 1918–1948* (Princeton, N.J., Princeton University Press, 1968) by Professor Dae-Sook Suh pretty much wrap up the subject? Does the field need another work on this subject?

My initial reaction was to answer "no" to these questions and proceed to other projects in progress. But the fact that the invitation requested a short monograph stopped me to ponder the questions further. Shorter work, of course, meant the distillation and compression of the vast amount of available data, but it could also mean the highlighting of significant events. Selection of what is significant and what is tangential also meant much more input of subjective interpretation. Couldn't the field "stand," if not benefit from, a shorter work of interpretive nature? Wouldn't the uninitiated welcome a short monograph setting forth the broad currents of the Korean Communist movement not encumbered by strings of unfamiliar names?

I obviously answered the last questions affirmatively; otherwise this monograph would have been written by someone else. This monograph, therefore, is my interpretation and summary of the history of the Korean Communist movement. Those already familiar with the works mentioned above will not find very much that is new or original in this monograph except the last two chapters dealing with the more recent events. Those interested in the details of the movement should also consult the larger volumes.

Writing an interpretive history in the wake of completing longer work on the same topic, however, allowed me to ponder some of the questions bypassed or tangentially referred to in earlier works. Since events in the movement have already been described in detail elsewhere and since I was not required to trace every action taken by those involved in the movement, I could address myself more to some of the questions that the participants, contemporary observers and latter-day analysts raised or failed to raise. Of course many questions have already been raised and answered in previous works. But I tried to do more of it as I reread works by myself and my colleagues. Other scholars in the field may not find the result very refreshing or interesting. But, as I attempted to answer some of the questions in this monograph, I found it necessary to grope for more data. In many cases, I could not find the information to satisfy my curiosity. It is common knowledge now, for example, that the petty bourgeois intelligentsia with some Japanese education predominated the socialist movement in Korea in the 1920s. We also know the background of some of the principal leaders. But very little is known about the background, motives, or thoughts of many of those who played very important roles. Lacking information about many of those involved in the leftwing oriented organizational movements in Korea in the early 1920s, one could only make inferences and educated guesses. It was quite frustrating to raise the simple question, "Who were the petty intelligentsia of Korea?" At best, our knowledge about the early phase of Korean communism is incomplete and partial. The same statement could be applied to the entire history of the Korean communist movement. I am sure that serious scholars in the field will agree with me when I say that much more work needs to be done on every phase of the Korean communist movement. Hopefully, more sources will become available to enable more detailed studies.

I wish to express my gratitude to George Ginsburgs for reading a portion of the manuscript for criticism; to Kay Dilks and Jacqueline Braun for typing the manuscript; and to editor Gene Tanke for helping make the text more readable.

CHONG-SIK LEE

Berwyn, Pa.
February 1977

Chapter 1

The Origins

If a card-carrying member of the Korean Workers' Party were asked in the 1970s to name the single factor that was most crucial in the rise and development of communism in Korea, he would undoubtedly cite the emergence of Kim Il-sŏng as a revolutionary fighter. Ever since 1926, when he was barely 15, Kim is supposed to have taken the "road to national salvation," upheld the banner of anti-Japanese armed struggle, and become the "savior of the anti-Japanese revolution." He is supposed to have founded the first Marxist-Leninist Party in Korea, defeated the "terrified Japanese imperialists," defeated American imperialism, and accomplished the socialist revolution in North Korea.[1] A Korean communist of the 1970s would be committing a cardinal sin if he were to attribute the rise of Korean communism to anything other than the leadership of President Kim.

The personality of Kim Il-sŏng did indeed play a dominant role in the development of communist Korea in the post-Korean War era, and to that extent, the North Korean claims have some merit. But those who take the broader perspective of the history of Korean communism, and examine the origins of the Korean communist movement, must cite other more impersonal factors. Indeed, earlier communist historians, up to the late 1950s, attributed the rise of Korean communism to socio-economic factors in Korea, particularly the rise of the industrial working class.[2] They noted the impoverishment of the farmers and the unbearable condition of the growing working class under Japanese colonial rule, and attempted to establish a causal relationship between these developments and the rise of Marxist study circles and the communist parties. This is, of course, a Marxist view of history, which stresses socio-economic factors as the prime motivator of political events.

Analysis of the participants in the communist movement indicates, however, the overwhelming significance of the Japanese colonization of Korea in 1905 and the strong reaction of the Koreans against it. There were undoubtedly some who were attracted to communism and recruited into the movement because of the communist call for the abolition of private property. But it would be quite accurate to say that the largest proportion of those who had either been affiliated with the movement or become a part of it before 1945 did so because they saw in the movement a way of restoring Korea's independence. In this sense, the Korean communist movement before 1945 was an offshoot of the nationalist movement, responding in part to the Leninist call for struggle against imperialism. Therefore, the history of the Korean communist movement before 1945, when Korea was freed from Japanese rule, must be seen in the context of Korea's struggle for independence.

It is tempting to ask whether Korea would have nurtured a significant communist movement if the Japanese had not taken over Korea. Judging from the experience of China and Japan in the 1920s, when significant numbers of young men participated in the communist movement, one must answer the question affirmatively. But, it is most likely that the communist movement in Korea would have suffered the same fate as in Japan. The conservative tradition was too strong, and the working class too meager. Unlike China, both Japan and Korea are too small for the communists to establish a guerrilla base in the hinterland. In any event, the movement would have attracted substantially different kinds of individuals, at least at the very beginning stage.

Being located on a small peninsula surrounded by sea on three sides and by a mountain mass in the north, the Korean people attained ethnic homogeneity and a sense of identity many centuries ago. Tribal states emerged before the Christian era, and by the first century, the Korean peninsula was ruled by three kingdoms, Koguryŏ, Paekche, and Silla. By the seventh century, the peninsula was unified under Silla, which was succeeded by Koryŏ (whence the English word Korea) in the tenth century and by the Yi-dynasty in the fourteenth. The Yi-dynasty Korea was called Chosŏn.

By the end of the nineteenth century, Yi-dynasty Korea was suffering from numerous problems that were traditionally thought to characterize the end of a dynastic cycle. But before the Koreans themselves were able to rejuvenate the society, it fell prey to the newly rising Japanese nation, which turned Korea into a protectorate in 1905 and annexed it in 1910.

These developments naturally aroused many patriots who organized armed bands to resist the Japanese, but by 1909, two years after it all began, the Japanese were able to suppress all resistance activity within Korea. Many of the die-hards fled across the northern border to Manchuria, where a large number of Koreans had immigrated since the late nineteenth century in search of farm lands. These Korean communities, along with those in eastern Siberia, became the strongholds of Korean resistance. The Japanese, in turn, placed all of Korea under a military rule, abolished all newspapers and magazines unfavorable to them, and prohibited all forms of political activity among the Koreans.

Many other Korean leaders in the meantime devoted their energy to private education and public lectures in the hope that they might strengthen the nation, but the Japanese suppressed these activities as well. Beginning in late 1910, the Japanese systematically arrested hundreds of Christian leaders in northwest Korea on a trumped-up charge of plotting the assassination of the Japanese governor-general; it put 123 of them through the most gruesome process of torture and interrogation. As the arrests and trials of these persons dragged on, anti-Japanese sentiments intensified, and many prominent figures not yet arrested found it prudent to go into exile abroad.

One of these exiles was Yi Tong-hwi (1873–1935), who played a key role in introducing communism to Korea. A product of Tanch'ŏn in south Hamgyŏng Province in the northeastern part of the peninsula, he had a personality to match the rugged mountainous terrain of his region. While serving as a lowly servant in the government at his home prefecture, at the age of eighteen, he is said to have lifted and thrown a burning brass stove at a governor accused of corrupt practices, and then fled to Seoul where he managed to enter the military academy. By 1905, when Japan turned Korea into a protectorate, he was a major in the army commanding a garrison battalion. In protest against the Japanese encroachment on Korea's sovereignty, he resigned his command and devoted himself to education, establishing private schools in the cities and villages of the central and northern part of the country. He also joined such other notable patriots as An Ch'ang-ho and Yi Kap to tour the land to encourage education and patriotism, and he played an important role in the establishment and operation of regional organizations dedicated to the propagation of education and patriotism.

His prominence, of course, subjected him to serious risks. In 1909, even before Japan officially annexed Korea, but after the Japanese had taken over the administration of "criminal justice" in July 1907, Yi was exiled by the Japanese to a remote island for six months; he was also briefly detained in connection with the alleged assassination plot against the governor-general in the winter of 1910 and was released after three months in jail. Upon release in the spring of 1911, he exiled himself to Chientao, in the southeastern part of Manchuria. Until he died in 1935 in Vladivostok, he was never to set foot on his native soil again.[3]

While the Chientao region on the north of the Tumen River was officially acknowledged to be a Chinese territory by a treaty signed between the Chinese and Japanese governments in September 1909, it was to all appearances an extension of Korea. Being adjacent to Korea and separated only by a narrow river, it was easy for the Korean immigrants to reach, while the Chinese immigrants needed to cross the vast plains and mountains of Manchuria to get there. It was not until 1928 that the railroad connection between Chilin, the major Chinese city in eastern Manchuria, and Tunhua, more than 100 miles west of Chientao, was completed, and it took another five years to connect Tunhua and Yenchi, the principal city of Chientao. It was natural, therefore, for the region to be populated predominantly by Koreans. Thus in 1912 there were 163,000 Koreans in the region but only 49,000 Chinese, a ratio of four Koreans to one Chinese.[4]

It was natural for Yi Tong-hwi to continue his activities among the Koreans in this region. In close cooperation with other Koreans already established there, he engaged in Christian evangelism, delivered patriotic lectures and speeches, and beginning in 1914, trained soldiers for the Chientao Korean National Association, a self-governing body of Koreans strongly dedicated to Korean nationalism. Being located within 100 miles of the Russian border, it was also natural for him to establish contacts with the Korean communities in the Maritime territory, which had another 40,000 to 50,000 Koreans. Thus in June 1917 we find Yi participating in the establishment of the Korean National Association in Vladivostok. Evidently he had decided that he was needed more in the Russian territory than in Manchuria at this juncture. Since he was an exile without a permanent home, and since his sole vocation lay in finding and nurturing the means to restore Korea's independence, he was ready to relocate himself whenever opportunities presented themselves.

The Bolshevik revolution did present such an opportunity. By the summer of 1917, some of the Bolshevik contingents were operating in the Maritime territory vying against the Social Democrats, Czarists, Czechs, the Japanese, and other elements of the Allied Expeditionary Forces. The Bolsheviks' position in eastern Siberia was still precarious, and they needed the support of every individual and every group that could be recruited to their cause. Since the Koreans possessed some organized strength in both political and military terms, it is only natural that the Bolsheviks turned to the Koreans. It would not have been difficult to accept the argument that to join the Bolshevik movement was the most effective method of supporting the liberation of Korea, because the Bolsheviks were dedicated to the cause of liberating the oppressed. The Bolsheviks promised to provide material support for the cause of Korean independence once they put the situation in Siberia under their control.

A man like Yi Tong-hwi would have required little persuasion to take up the Bolshevik offer. It was the first time since Korea was conquered by the Japanese that any political group from abroad offered to help the cause of the Koreans. In 1905 the Korean emperor had desperately tried to solicit the intercession of the United States government to prevent the Japanese encroachment, but to no avail. In 1907 two emissaries of the Korean emperor, both close comrades of Yi Tong-hwi, had tried to plead the case of Korea at the Hague Conference, but with the same results. The Koreans had seen a flash of hope in the Republican revolutionaries of China in 1911, but the revolutionaries under Sun Yat-sen were soon driven from their homeland and sought refuge in Japan and elsewhere. In contrast, the Bolsheviks were confronting the Koreans with an offer for help in return for Korean support in their moments of need. This was a godsend the Koreans could not afford to refuse. The fact that one of the most formidable enemies facing the Bolsheviks in Siberia consisted of Japanese troops would have precipitated the decision. As Yi later told one of his colleagues in the nationalist movement:

> Since the Russian Revolution, the Bolsheviks have been gradually coming to Siberia and Mongolia. I have been in the Siberia area for a long time and I know a good many Russians. I hope to win cooperation from

> them. . . . To bring the matter of Korean independence before the League of Nations is one way, but even if we fail, we must continue our efforts. . . . Although we have some relations with the southern Chinese group of Sun Yat-sen, we cannot anticipate any great assistance. It is the same with France and England. The United States did not even join the League. To join with the Russian Bolsheviks is therefore the only shortcut.[5]

It was in this frame of mind that Yi organized the Korean People's Socialist Party (Hanin Sahoe-dang) in Khavarovsk in June 1918 with a handful of like-minded people. On April 25, 1919, the same group meeting in the outskirts of Vladivostok decided to send representatives to Moscow to meet with the central Soviet government and the newly created Third International. The three delegates from Vladivostok were warmly received and provided some funds. They in turn, signed an agreement with the new Soviet government pledging their party to work for the liberation of Korea and the espousal of the communist cause.[6]

Thus, the organization of the first Korean "socialist party" was the result of the nationalists seeking foreign assistance rather than acting on ideological convictions. One could argue, of course, that Yi and his cohorts may have gone through an ideological conversion between 1917 and 1919. But, considering the language barrier and the confusing circumstances in which they operated, one could not expect the old revolutionaries to have read or learned much about the tenets of communism beyond the most rudimentary principles. Furthermore, Yi was clearly not a philosophically inclined intellectual. Nor was he a man of worker's origin who might be imbued with "proletarian consciousness." He was a man of action with a deep commitment to Korean independence. In spite of his title as the chairman of the Korean Socialist Party, he was a man far removed in orientation from such individuals as Li Ta-chao and Ch'en Tu-hsiu, who later spearheaded the Chinese communist movement. One must therefore trace the origins of Korean communism to the Korean passion for the recovery of their national independence.

The Bolshevik leaders in Moscow would have been apprised of these facts, but this did not pose any serious problem for them. As stated before, their immediate concern in Siberia was in recruiting any armed group that could strengthen the Bolshevik struggle against their enemies. The ideologies of the allies, in this context, were of little concern. Far more important, as Lenin had recognized as early as 1916, were "the more revolutionary elements in the bourgeois-democratic movement for national liberation" in such backward countries as China, Persia, and Turkey. Lenin called for support and assistance on the part of European socialists for their rebellion, and "if need be, their revolutionary war against imperialist powers that oppress them."[7] He felt that only the bourgeoisie was capable of leading revolutionary action against foreign capitalism in what he called the semi-colonial and colonial countries, and that its success would depend primarily on arousing the millions of peasants to active participation.[8] He had no illusions concerning the development of Marxism in the Far East, and he was willing to offer support to the nationalist bourgeoisie. Therefore, in June 1920, when the Korean Provisional Government in Shanghai—under Premier Yi Tong-hwi—sent Han Hyŏng-gwŏn to Moscow to seek financial and other forms of assistance, Lenin was favorably disposed. He is reported to have told the Korean emissary: "I know full well that without destroying Japanese imperialism and militarism the freedom and happiness of the Asian peoples cannot be attained. In Korea, a proletarian social revolution is not necessary at this time. It is the time only for a national revolution, an independence movement. We will therefore support the Korean independence movement with all of our strength."[9] Lenin subsequently authorized a payment of two million gold rubles as an initial grant to the Korean cause, and reports about a treaty between the Lenin government and the Korean Provisional Government were circulated soon after.[10]

Thus even if Yi Tong-hwi had not organized a "socialist party," Lenin would have been receptive to his pleas for support. But when he and his cohorts presented themselves as "socialists," there is no doubt that Lenin encouraged them to organize a revolutionary (or proletarian) nucleus to propagate communist ideas. After all, the Bolsheviks had nothing to lose.

What was Yi Tong-hwi's subsequent record as a communist leader? To what extent did the Korean nationalist movement gain from the alliance with the Bolsheviks? Was the overall record satisfying to Lenin and his successors?

In spite of numerous difficulties he encountered, Yi and his group cast their nets widely among the Koreans in Siberia, Manchuria, and China proper, carrying out brisk propaganda and organizational activities. While still serving as the premier of the Provisional Government, Yi organized the Korean Communist Party (Koryŏ Kangsan-dang) in

Shanghai by gathering a nucleus of associates in the nationalist movement. Since Shanghai has become a major center of the Korean exiles after the nationwide demonstration movement in Korea in March 1919, there were several hundred highly politicized Koreans who might be recruited into his cause. The Soviet pledge for support of the Korean cause and the initial payment of 400,000 gold rubles by the Soviet government (200,000 rubles to come later) activated the Korean leaders, who had received no aid from a foreign source since their country had been taken over by the Japanese. Letters and agents were dispatched, propaganda materials translated, printed, and distributed. Armed bands were organized and trained. Contacts were made and funds distributed to would-be organizers of other Asians, particularly the Chinese and Japanese. While the latter venture brought no tangible results, by the fall of 1921 Japanese authorities estimated that some 150,000 Koreans in Manchuria and Siberia had been influenced by "Bolshevik propaganda."[11] In August 1922, the Japanese authorities reported the total number of party members under Yi Tong-hwi to be 6,812 including 2,750 full members and 4,020 candidate members.[12] While these reports may be exaggerated, this record must be considered a success by any standard. It should be noted for comparison that the Chinese Communist Party had only 950 members in early 1925, four years after its founding.[13]

But the movement under Yi faced many problems that did not augur well for its future. First, the speed with which the "party" expanded in its membership, and the ideological outlook of the top party leaders we can identify, suggests that most of the members were not genuine ideological converts, but were interested instead in sharing the spoils from Moscow or in fighting for the cause of Korean independence with Soviet aid. Not only did the leaders not undergo a deep ideological transformation, but the party did not possess facilities for training cadres with knowledge and ability to convert others. It is significant to note that while there are numerous reports concerning the establishment of military training centers, there is not a single report concerning study circles of communist literature organized by Yi's group, not to mention the establishment of cadre schools. All the 6,800 party members were thus instant converts—people who became "communists" after listening to a lecture or two on rudimentary principles of communism or reading a pamphlet or two issued by the party. More likely, they were Yi's followers in various localities who shared the belief that the party roster should be swelled in order to receive continued support from the Bolsheviks. In this situation, the party's strength would be contingent upon continued Soviet support for the Korean cause as well as the supply of funds.

The second problem was the feud between Yi Tong-hwi and another group of Korean communists with their headquarters in Irkutsk, Siberia. There were several thousand Koreans in this region, and its being a region far removed from the Korean border, most of the Koreans there had either become naturalized citizens of Russia or had been there long enough to become acculturated to the foreign culture. Thus, these Koreans shared a considerably different outlook from the recent exiles in Siberia, Manchuria, and China, the kind of exiles represented by Yi. While the recent exiles' motive in joining the Bolshevik ranks was in gaining Korean independence, most of those in Irkutsk who had joined the Bolshevik ranks as armed fighters or party members were more attuned to the basic tenets of communist ideology, Korean independence being only a matter of secondary importance. These Korean-Russians had organized the Korean Department of the Irkutsk branch of the Bolshevik Party in January 1918, and as the Bolsheviks expanded into eastern Siberia, they began to assert their right to organize the Koreans there, and changed their group's name in September 1919 to All-Russian Korean Communist Party. The chairman was Kim Ch'ŏl-hun. Henceforth, the All-Russian Party was to have full jurisdiction over the communist movement among the Koreans in Siberia, including the territories previously covered by the Yi group.[14]

The Irkutsk group had a chance to translate its claims into action almost as soon as it had changed the name of its organization. Within the same month, Yi's emissary, Pak Chin-sun, reached Irkutsk from Moscow, where he had been dispatched as a representative of Yi's Korean Socialist Party. Pak was carrying a considerable sum of money granted by the Comintern (some sources say 4 million rubles, but this is undoubtedly exaggeration). Knowing this, the Irkutsk group forced Pak to turn over the funds claiming that Yi's group was under the jurisdiction of the All-Russian Party and hence the use of the funds should be determined by it.[15] The Irkutsk group could have argued also that Yi Tong-hwi was no longer engaged in the socialist movement because he had already left for Shanghai in the late summer of that year to assume the premiership of the Provisional Government in Shanghai, a government in exile created by the nationalist leaders abroad. In any event, the reaction of Yi's group to this outrage can be easily surmised.

The situation was exacerbated by two other factors: the prejudice of an important Russian Bolshevik in Irkutsk to the Irkutsk group, and the dispute over the disposition of the Moscow funds.

Boris Shumiatsky (1886–?) had been active for the Bolshevik cause in Siberia as early as 1905, and after the October Revolution, he became the chairman of the Central Executive Committee of the Soviets of Siberia and a member of the Siberian Bureau (later Far Eastern Bureau) of the Central Committee of Russian Communist Party. Later, he was also given the title of Plenipotentiary of People's Commissariat of Foreign Affairs for Siberia and Head of the Comintern's Far Eastern Secretariat in Irkutsk.[16] Until 1922, when he was sent to Persia as Soviet ambassador and trade representative, Shumiatsky's power and authority in Siberia were unquestionable.

As an old Bolshevik dedicated to the cause of expanding his party in Siberia, and being in close communication with the Koreans in Irkutsk, Shumiatsky evidently accepted the position of the Irkutsk Koreans uncritically. The leaders in Moscow were clearly taking a broader perspective in aiding Yi Tong-hwi and the Provisional Government, but Shumiatsky seems to have been oblivious to this. Either he disagreed with the Moscow policy or he thought Moscow's trust in Yi misplaced, particularly in view of Yi's claim that he was a communist leader. In any event, Shumiatsky evidently approved the Irkutsk group's "confiscation" of funds from Pak Chin-sun in September 1919. In May 1921, when the Comintern's Far Eastern Secretariat (headed by Shumiatsky!) convened a meeting of the two groups in Irkutsk ostensibly to resolve the conflict between them, Shumiatsky stood behind the Irkutsk group. Shumiatsky's attitude intensified the conflict among the Koreans, or more accurately between the Koreans and Korean-Russians; Shumiatsky fortified the Irkutsk group's position, but the Yi group was not willing to yield.

What effect, if any, the inter-group hostility had on recruiting followers cannot be determined, but there were some obvious adverse effects. In June 1921, a battle broke out at Alekseyevsk, now Svobodny, some eighty miles north of Blagoveshchensk, between the armed forces of the Irkutsk group and recent arrivals from Manchuria supporting the Yi group. The issue involved was the old one; the Irkutsk group, supported by the Far Eastern Secretariat of the Comintern, insisted that all Korean troops in Siberia were to be united under its command. This position was rejected by the new arrivals as a scheme to gain control over

Korean military forces. The resistance of the Yi forces was of no avail; several hundreds of their troops were killed, more than a thousand wounded, and a large number were sent to prison or put to forced labor in lumbering camps. This shameful incident engraved a deep scar on the Korean communist and nationalist movements.

Another effect of the feud was the stoppage of funds from Moscow. As noted earlier, Lenin had promised two million rubles to the Provisional Government, and Han Hyŏng-gwŏn had received the initial payment of 400,000 rubles. He handed the seven boxes of gold coins to Kim Rip, a close associate of Yi Tong-hwi and a founder of the "socialist party," at Omsk, and headed back to Moscow for the remainder of the funds, but when he reached Moscow, the Soviet leaders had serious misgivings about Yi Tong-hwi and the Provisional Government. Obviously the Irkutsk group had filed damaging reports about Yi. The Provisional Government in Shanghai, for which the funds had been intended, was also in serious trouble because of internal dissension, Japanese harassment, and general disillusionment with the lack of success. All of this must have been reported by Grigorii Voitinsky, another leading Comintern agent, who arrived in Shanghai in the spring of 1920. In any event, Han was given only 200,000 gold rubles after some four months of delay, and he returned to Shanghai only in November 1922. The Koreans were never to receive the remaining 1,400,000 gold rubles pledged to them.

Even the 600,000 gold rubles (approximately 300,000 United States dollars at this time) might have had an enormously stimulating effect on the Provisional Government, as well as on the communist movement under Yi Tong-hwi, but this was not to be. For whatever reasons, Kim Rip did not submit the 400,000 gold rubles to the Provisional Government, nor did he share the funds with very many colleagues either in the nationalist or the communist camp. Some of the money (80,000 yen, the equivalent of 80,000 gold rubles) went to Yi's former colleagues now in Korea and was spent on lectures and publications of liberal contents. Lesser amounts (one source says 20,000 yen to the Japanese and 10,000 yen to the Chinese) were spent to seed communist movements in China and Japan, but without any result. The remaining funds were presumably spent on the organizational and propaganda activities described above, or as some accounts have it, for Kim's personal use. When the news about the funds finally broke out, other leaders in the Provisional Government as well as those in the communist group were naturally incensed. But Kim offered no accounting or explanation, and Yi stood by him.

These events alienated Yi not only from the other nationalists but also from many of his cohorts in the communist party. About half the members, including such influential figures as Yŏ Un-hyŏng, An Pyŏng-ch'an, Kim Man-gyŏm, and Cho Tong-ho, went to Irkutsk to join the communists there in May 1921, and established the Shanghai branch of the Irkutsk party in July.

Voitinsky, who had established a close relationship with Kim Man-gyŏm and Yŏ Un-hyŏng, provided some financial support to this new group. Thus, in spite of abundant funds, or because of them, Yi's forces lost the most precious assets in their possession, namely the prestige of Yi Tong-hwi and articulate and influential second-echelon leaders. Having enlisted these dissidents from Shanghai, the Irkutsk group became invincible. In addition to the propaganda and organizational activities carried out in Siberia from Irkutsk, the Shanghai branch translated and printed propaganda materials for distribution and organized a Communist Youth League, or Comsomol, with a library and study circles. The leaders of the Comsomol were Pak Hŏn-yŏng, Kim T'ae-yŏn (better known by his alias Kim Tan-ya), and Yim Wŏn-gŭn, a trio that came to play very important roles later in the communist movement within Korea. Pak, for example, emerged in Seoul in 1945 as the undisputed leader of the communist movement throughout Korea. Yŏ Un-hyŏng, in turn, emerged as the most widely acclaimed progressive leader in Korea in 1945.

In terms of the number of party members enlisted, the Irkutsk group fell somewhat behind the Yi group, but since the quality of party members is unknown, the numbers alone cannot become a criteria for judging the accomplishments of either group. The Japanese authorities reported the membership data of the Irkutsk group as of August 1922 to be 4,433 including 3,580 candidate members.[17] It is evident that the Irkutsk group was more rigorous in enforcing rules concerning admission to full membership. Compared to 2,750 full members in the Yi group, there were only 850 full members in the Irkutsk group.

These impressive statistics notwithstanding, the Comintern was gravely concerned about the factional strife among the Korean communists, and a number of attempts were made to reconcile the differences. Shumiatsky, as noted earlier, was sent off to Persia sometime in 1922, and the Yi group would have been relieved, but by then too much had transpired between the two groups and emotions had become too tangled for reconciliation to be achieved. Finally, in December 1922, the two warring parties were ordered to be dissolved, to be replaced by Comintern's Far East Area Committee's Korea Bureau (Korburo) to be located in Vladivostok. It was to consist of five Koreans selected from both groups and to be headed by Voitinsky.

The Korburo began its activities in January 1923, but there is no indication that the affair was taken very seriously by anyone involved. There is no sign that large amounts of funds were allocated for its activities. Two of the five Bureau members found it more urgent to go to Shanghai, where the National Representatives Conference (to be described later) was being held. Voitinsky is said to have left for China. According to Chŏng Chae-dal, who served as the principal staff of the Bureau, his main tasks were to prepare the roster of the Korean communists in Siberia, to obtain jobs for unemployed communists, and to prepare for his planned trip to Korea where the Bureau was hoping to launch a communist party.

The low profile taken by the Korburo was, of course, not simply due to the insoluble conflict among the Koreans. For all practical purposes, the era of communist movement among the exiles under the Bolsheviks ended in late 1922. As the Bolsheviks consolidated their power in eastern Siberia, and as the Japanese completed their troop withdrawal from Siberia in October 1922, there was no longer any reason for the Bolsheviks to harbor the Korean nationalist troops on the Soviet soil. The Soviet government began its longdrawn and delicate negotiations with the Japanese on troop withdrawal, trade, fishery, and the future relations between the two countries since August 1921, and it was not deemed to be in the interest of the Soviet Union to overly stimulate the Japanese. All Korean troops within Soviet territory except those constituting an integral part of the Soviet armed forces were to be disarmed. All the Korean revolutionaries, other than those belonging to the Russian Communist Party, were to be expelled. The establishment of the Korburo with a charge to organize and direct communist movement within Korea was the only concession—or risk—the Soviet leaders were willing to take. Communism was a universal or cosmopolitan doctrine transcending nationalities, but the interest of the "fatherland of international socialism" must be protected first. The Soviet leaders could say, of course, that they had provided enough assistance to the Koreans, and owed them no apologies.

Purely Korean movement within Soviet territory, of course, quickly disappeared as most Korean communists were absorbed into the Russian party. The movement in Shanghai also ebbed and faded into obscurity; Yi was in the Korburo in Vladivostok, and Kim Rip was assassinated in January 1922. Most of the other nationalists and proto-communists in Shanghai and elsewhere were absorbed during the National Representatives' Conference held in Shanghai between January and May 1923. This was a conference of the leaders of a broad spectrum of Korean exile groups abroad being financed by the 200,000 gold rubles brought back by Han Hyŏng-gwŏn from Moscow. There are signs that the Comintern had placed considerable hope in resuscitating the united front of Korean nationalists and communists through this conference, but that unity was not attained. While the majority, including most of Yi's group and some of the Irkutsk group leaders in Shanghai, advocated the reform of the Provisional Government that had been established in 1919, a stubborn minority insisted on starting a new political institution. Subsequently, in June, this minority drew up a plan for a new government and went to Vladivostok in the hope of announcing its establishment there, but the Soviet government expelled some forty of this group and sent them back to Shanghai. As the prominent leaders in Shanghai and Irkutsk faded into the background, the communist movement in Manchuria also quietly dissipated. The first era of Korean communism came to a close.

Chapter 2

Intelligentsia and Communism in Korea

When the Comintern leaders, disgruntled with the Korean exiles abroad, cast their eyes to Korea around 1922, a broad current of socialism had already stimulated the interest of young iconoclasts. Since March 1, 1919, when thousands of Koreans participated in the nationwide demonstrations against the harsh rule of the Japanese, the country has been undergoing significant changes. The Japanese colonial government discontinued its policy of absolute rule imposed on Korea since 1910, and initiated its "culture policy" under which the Koreans were allowed considerable freedom of press, publication, assembly, and organization. While the colonial police continued to impose more stringent restrictions on these activities than in Japan, there was a world of difference in the political atmosphere in Korea before and after 1919. Until May 1925, when the Law on Public Peace Maintenance (Chian ijihō) was promulgated in Korea, outlawing all activities connected with organizations that "purport to change the polity (kokutai) or to deny the private property system," the Koreans were allowed considerable freedom. The moderate movement of the older nationalists since 1919 having failed to produce a dramatic result, more and more of the younger generation were attracted to the new currents of thoughts being introduced through Japan. It became fashionable for the young to be involved in the radical movements which came to be identified as a mark of a progressive intelligentsia. Numerous coteries were organized to study and propagate socialist thoughts. Under this situation, the overall strength of the left-wing movement within the anti-Japanese nationalist camp gained significantly between 1921 and 1925. While there were only a score or so of Marxist-oriented intelligentsia in Korea in 1921, and they were barely recognized as components of the anti-Japanese camp, the left-wing movement came to dominate the socio-political scene by 1924.

Whereas the nationalist movement abroad (described in the previous chapter) and the non-Marxist nationalist movement within Korea were dominated by the relatively well-known and established figures of the society, the Marxist movement was led mostly by the young and the unknown. They were also long on passion and determination and short on intellect or theoretical training. Typically, a Korean radical was an individual who had gone to Japan for higher education but interrupted his education for lack of money to become a political activist. Later, in the 1930s, a few college professors joined the ranks of the communist movement, but until then, it was rare to find a university graduate among Korean communists. Most of the Koreans who could either afford an uninterrupted regular schooling or were unaffected by the radical current sweeping the Japanese labor and intellectual circles were attracted to the moderate wing of the nationalist movement, or in many cases, simply stayed away from the political arena. These facts may explain the remarkable lack of theoretical disputes among the Korean communists, whereas such disputes were common among their Chinese and Japanese counterparts. The Korean communists, on the other hand, had more than their share of factional wrangles. The fact that the Korean movement lacked luminaries of Li Ta-ch'ao's or Ch'en Tu-hsiu's caliber undoubtedly had an effect also.

Take, for example, the case of Kim Tu-jŏn, better known by his alias Kim Yak-su, who played a dominant role among the Marxist-oriented Korean intelligentsia in both Japan and Korea in the early years. A man born in Seoul around 1893 or 1894, he had gone to Tokyo in 1915 with the hope of joining the Japanese Military Academy. Having been refused admission, he and his friends decided to go to Peking to seek admission to the Military Academy there. On the way, however, he had his group's travel and schooling funds stolen and was stalled in the border city of Antung. By the time he received an additional sum from home, he was absorbed in the idea of organizing in the Chilin Province in Manchuria a village of armed farmers who might be mobilized later for the cause of Korean independence. But this plan did not materialize.

Finally in 1919, in the wake of the March First movement, he returned to Korea, and then proceeded to Tokyo. There, he participated in the organization of the Friends Society of the Working Korean Students in Tokyo (Tong-gyŏng Chosŏn Kohaksaeng Tong-u-hoe) which was launched in January 1920, with some 300 persons attending the inaugural meeting. Like many other Korean students there, he also associated with prominent Japanese anarchists and communists, and under their influence, organized the Black Current Society (Huk-to-hoe), an anarchist-communist organization, in November 1921. A month later he broke with his anarchist friends and in January 1923 he and some sixty friends organized the North Star Society (Puk-sŏng-hoe), a Marxist group. Most of his cohorts were Korean students working their way through schools and colleges in Tokyo.[1]

Another more or less typical case is Kim Nak-jun, better known by his alias Kim Ch'an. His father was a local leader of a pro-Japanese organization, Il-chin-hoe, which had been active just before the Japanese annexation of Korea, and was appointed a prefectural governor. After finishing the eighth grade, Kim Ch'an enrolled in the Medical Training Center operated by the colonial government in 1912, but quickly withdrew from it to go to Tokyo where he entered the College department (Senmonbu) of Meiji University. After a year, however, he went to Chientao in Manchuria, returning to Tokyo in 1915, where he worked as a house boy, in the meantime attending Meiji University and reading communist literature. Within a year, we find him in another private university, Chū-ō University, but he withdrew from it two years later without graduating. Meanwhile, he traveled to Vladivostok in August 1919 and to Irkutsk in September 1921. Like Kim Yak-su, he was a founding member of the Friends Society and of the Black Current Society. We then see him traveling to Manchuria, Siberia, and Korea, establishing contacts with various communists there.[2] Kim Ch'an was to play an important role in the Korean communist movement.

It was natural that these activists with many political and economic grievances should have been drawn to the new wave of anarchism and communism that swept Japanese labor and intellectual circles. Many prominent Japanese anarchist and communist leaders, including Ōsugi Sakae, Iwasa Sakutarō, Sakai Toshihiko, and Sano Manabu, had Korean proteges. Other Japanese leaders, such as Fuse Tatsuji and Kitahara Tatsuo, visited Korea in August 1923 on behalf of Kim Yak-su and his group to participate in a lecture tour stopping in such cities as Seoul,

Pyongyang, Kwangju, Taegu, Masan, Chinju, and Kimhae.[3] Thus the Japanese radicals became an important source of inspiration and influence for the Korean radical movement. The fact that there were several hundred Korean students in Japan at the secondary level or above, and that many of them had less than adequate means of support, exerted a great impact.[4] The large and steady influx of other Koreans into Japan also had its effects. At the end of 1910, there had been only 250 Koreans in Japan; the number increased to over 22,000 in 1918, and swelled to 243,000 ten years later. As to be expected, most of these immigrants were South Korean farmers who could not eke out a living under the colonial government and decided to take their chances in Japan. It should be noted, however, that not all the radically affected intelligentsia were poor and struggling students. While Kim Yak-su's family background is unknown, he was amply supported by a wealthy patriot of Milyang, South Kyŏngsang province, Hong Saeng-gu. He also drew liberally on the wealth of his blood-brother Yi Yŏ-sŏng, whose father was a rich landlord.[5] Without these funds the young radicals could not dream the big dreams, such as organizing armed villages, publishing journals, conducting lecture tours, or simply traveling from one region of East Asia to another.

It will be difficult to determine the exact date or manner in which the first messenger of Marxist tidings entered Korea. Since the Japanese radicals began to publish their journals before Japan annexed Korea in 1910, and since many Koreans were already engaged in communist activities abroad after the Russian Revolution, it is reasonable to assume that some individuals within Korea had already come into contact with socialist thoughts before 1920. But the first Marxist-inclined action taken within Korea by the new intelligentsia cannot be traced earlier than April of 1920, when the Korean Labor Mutual Aid Society (Chosŏn Nodong Kongje-hoe) was established in Seoul. If the Marxist intellectuals—if they could indeed be called such—did play any role in it, however, it would have been very minor. Of the 17 officers elected by some 600 persons attending the inauguration conference, only 3 were of socialist leaning. The Society was sponsored by the bourgeoisie—businessmen, medical doctors, lawyers, newspaper publishers, and religious leaders—and the statement of principles adopted by the inauguration conference invoked God's justice, heavenly will, the usual traditional sanctions. The platform, in turn, called for encouragement of savings, advancement of education, improvement of workers' character, and relief from calamities. The socialist elements in the Society, however, did begin to make themselves felt soon after. The topics of lectures delivered on May 1 by these men (Kim Myŏng-sik and Chŏng T'ae-sin)[6] were "Contradictions in the Class Society" and "The Labor Union and the Contemporary World Situation." Another socialist, Yu Chin-hui, a graduate of the Kyŏngsŏng Medical College in Seoul and a practicing doctor, published a newspaper editorial on the same date sharply criticizing the patronizing attitude of the Society's sponsors.

By 1921 the socialists were more active. A few more Marxist intelligentsia entered the Mutual Aid Society's executive department and began to exert more influence. In May, three "delegates" from Korea (Yi Pong-su, Chu Chong-gŏn, and Yu Chin-hui) went to Shanghai to attend Yi Tong-hwi's party's Representative Conference, returning to Korea in July. Kim Ch'ŏl-su is also said to have returned to Korea from Shanghai in the same month with Yi Tong-hwi's funds, although some sources say that it was Yi Pong-su who carried the money.[7]

It was in January 1922, however, when the first known public announcement of the intent to carry out class struggle in Korea was issued by Kim Yak-su and his cohorts of the Friends Society of Tokyo.[8] The Friends Society declared that henceforth it would no longer be a relief agency of the working students and laborers but would engage in the new mission of class struggle. Within the same month, another coterie of returned students from Tokyo established the Proletarian League (Musanja Tong-maeng-hoe) in Seoul with the announced aim of promoting the rights of the proletariat. Reflecting the "new mood," the colonial police did not suppress any of these activities. The organizers of the League were those who had previously returned to Korea and they were occupying leading positions in the press, youth societies, and labor organizations that were rapidly spreading throughout Korea.[9] The more recent returnees and the earlier returnees maintained close contacts among themselves, and taken together, they constituted an important segment of the "new intelligentsia." Evidently they found an eager audience. The first lecture sponsored by the League on December 22, 1922, in Seoul drew some 1,500 persons including some 200 cobblers, one of the speakers being a cobbler himself. All the speakers used radical language to attack the capitalist system.[10]

As noted earlier, Kim Yak-su and others conducted a lecture tour of various cities accompanied by the two Japanese radicals in August 1923. In October, the group established the Construction Society (Kŏnsŏlsa), attracting 130 persons to its inaugural meeting. In November, the same group established the North Wind Society (Puk-p'ung-hoe) and absorbed the members of the Construction Society. This was to become the Korean headquarters of the North Star Society in Tokyo.

At about the same time, in July 1923, Kim Ch'an and his cohorts—including some members of the Proletarian League—established the New Thought Study Society (Shin Sasang Yŏnguhoe) ostensibly to study "the torrents of the new thoughts" being introduced into Korea. But this was not the full story. Kim Ch'an, who had been to Vladivostok in the spring of that year, had established contacts with the Korburo there and had agreed on a mission to establish a communist party within Korea. Since June, Kim and his cohorts (including Kim Yak-su and Yi Pong-su) actively recruited secret members and organized Korburo cells in various newspapers, youth organizations, and intellectual circles. In effect, Kim Ch'an built a bridge between the bourgeoning intellectual movement originating in Japan and the organizational interest of the Korburo, which represented the Comintern as well as the Shanghai and Irkutsk factions. By the fall of 1924, approximately 130 members were recruited and cell organizations were formed in various major cities of Korea. Steady efforts were also made to maneuver the labor, farmer, and youth organizations under the direction of the Korburo. Because most of the secret members were in leading positions in these organizations, such efforts succeeded relatively easily. The New Thoughts Study Society was renamed the Tuesday Society (Hwayohoe) on November 19, 1924, the birthday of Karl Marx, because the day happened to be Tuesday, and it was decided that the Society would change its orientation from study to action. This perhaps reflects the growing confidence of the young intelligentsia. The Tuesday Society maintained close relationship with the North Wind Society, and in March 1925, the leaders of the two groups agreed on a merger. The Korean Communist Party (Chosŏn Kongsandang), established on April 17, 1925, was the result.

Thus the Korean Communist Party (KCP) was established by the petty bourgeois intelligentsia who had been stimulated by radical Japanese intellectuals. To the extent that the Russian, Chinese, Japanese, and other communist parties were the creatures of small numbers of aroused intellectuals, the KCP created in 1925 fits the established pattern. But the task of organizing the proletariat and leading them to the revolution remained a distant hope. The Russian Bolsheviks had been more fortunate. They were able to manipulate the chaotic political and economic conditions in their country in the aftermath of the disastrous war. The Chinese communists, on the other hand, had the advantage of operating in a country torn by rebellions, foreign invasion, and political chaos. But, like the Japanese communists, the Korean communists possessed none of these advantages. The Japanese colonial government was firmly entrenched and it possessed a very efficient and effective police system. It was determined to wipe out all forms of subversion, and it had the ability to do so. The odds against Korean revolutionaries—both the communist and non-communist varieties—were therefore enormous.

A Marxist analysis of the stage of economic development in Korea would also have shown the enormity of the problems confronting Korean communists. Korean capitalism was still very much in the incipient stage of development, very much akin to that of China. Factories were only just developing (2,087 in 1920, 3,499 in 1923), and the number of wage-earning workers was minuscule.[11] Should the Korean communists, as the Mensheviks argued before the Bolshevik revolution, help bring about a bourgeois revolution in Korea which could involve the vigorous and even leading participation of the proletariat? Or should the Korean communists work toward the building of a revolutionary force that could strike simultaneously against the "feudal" forces, the capitalists, and the Japanese empire? If so, how should this revolutionary force be forged? Should the peasants be enlisted or should the proletariat do it alone? How should the fact that Korea is a Japanese colony be accounted for in the KCP's revolutionary strategy? Should the Korean communists work toward a coalition with the nationalists according to the current Comintern line, or should they try to take an independent course, as most of the Chinese communists advocated in the early 1920s?

These, one would think, are the questions that the aspiring communists of the early 1920s should have discussed. Honest difference of opinion could emerge because every course of action contained risks and raised important theoretical questions. The implications of each alternative needed to be understood before decisions were made. At least by the time the KCP was established, the communist leaders needed to have deliberated on these questions and formulated a set of theses. It could serve as a basis for long-range planning and as a source from which later strategies and tactics could be drawn. As far as it can be ascertained, however, there is no indication that such debate ever took place. The Korean communists were simply willing to let the Comintern and their Japanese mentors do the thinking for them. They were too preoccupied with the organizational tasks of bringing various coteries of men together, distributing "power positions" among various factions, and recruiting new members. Why was this so?

The absence of any meaningful debate is probably a reflection of the caliber of men involved in the movement. As noted earlier, most of these men joined the revolutionary ranks before they even graduated from an institution of higher learning. Although they are likely to have engaged in theoretical discourses in their coteries, one suspects that they were still studying the basic tenets of Marxism-Leninism rather than attempting to apply these theories creatively to the concrete situation in Korea. The names of such organizations as the New Thought Study Society (which could also be translated as the Society for the Study of New Thoughts) indeed had accurately described the nature of the activities undertaken. While there is no doubt that they were influenced by the new ideology, it is doubtful that they sufficiently mastered the theories to be creative with it. The Korean Marxist intelligentsia of this period thus consisted more of followers and activists than of thinkers. The Korean communists never developed the counterparts of Fukumoto Kazuo, Yamakawa Hitoshi, Li Li-san, or Mao Tse-tung. Instead, there were Fukumotoists, Yamakawaists, Li Lisanists and so on.

As long as the strategies enunciated by the Comintern or spawned by Japanese mentors were appropriate to the situation in Korea, the lack of intellectual and strategic autonomy did not constitute a serious problem. But the Comintern was an international organization, and its strategies were not always geared to the objective conditions in Korea. Indeed, the Comintern may have been appalled at the thought that the Korean communists were adopting a policy line devised in Japan. The Korean communists occasionally paid a high price for their lack of autonomy, as we shall see later.

The Comintern's policy as of 1924, in its own words, was as follows: "Besides strengthening the Communist Party, the chief task of our comrades in Korea should consist in furthering the formation and unification of the pure labor organizations, and in substituting revolutionary-minded comrades for the Right Wing elements in the organizations. In the purely Nationalist movement, the Communists should work for the establishment of a united front of the National-revolutionary struggle."[12]

When the formation of the KCP in Seoul was reported, the Comintern directed the KCP to "give first priority to the national liberation struggle by uniting with the workers, peasants, and all other working elements: handicraftsmen, the intelligentsia, and the petty and middle bourgeoisie."[13] According to Otto Kuusinen, one of the principal Comintern leaders, joint discussions were conducted at this time (probably with Korean delegates) on the question of forming in Korea a national revolutionary party of the Kuomintang type.[14] Thus the tasks assigned were: (1) to strengthen the party, (2) to work among the labor unions, and (3) to establish a united front with the nationalists. Given the aspirations of the Korean communists at this period, these are the tasks they would have readily agreed to—although given their radical inclinations and their animosities toward the nationalists, they were not likely to have chosen the last assignment on their own.

The task of "furthering the formation and unification of the pure labor organizations and substituting revolutionary-minded comrades for the Right Wing elements in the organizations" progressed relatively well. Those leaders who had launched the Proletarian Comrades League succeeded by October 1922 in dissolving the bourgeois-dominated Mutual Aid Society. Within the same month, they established the Korean Labor Federation (Chosŏn Nodong Yŏnmaeng-hoe) with a platform that called for the construction of a new society and unity based on "class consciousness." The federation placed under it 13 labor unions and mutual aid societies in various regions of Korea, the total membership being some 20,000. The federation began to intervene in labor strikes on behalf of labor unions and directed strikes and demonstrations to celebrate May Day.[15]

Most of the strikes, however, were not planned but spontaneous. Fraternal organizations of workers, beginning with those of miners, had existed in Korea since the latter part of the Yi dynasty (1392–1910), and the first organization bearing the name of Labor Union was organized in 1898 by forty-seven stevedores in Sŏngjin.[16] The first collective action by the miners that led to a violent riot erupted in 1888,[17] and the first modern form of labor strike was conducted in 1898 by stevedores in Mokp'o.[18]

The momentum created by the organizers of the Korean Labor Federation was carried by others in different localities. Thus, three labor groups in South Kyŏngsang province launched a federation movement in January 1924, which led to the establishment in March of the South

Korean Labor Federation consisting of ninety organizations. Negotiations continued, and in April 1924, the Korean Labor and Farmer Federation was organized in Seoul by 295 representatives of 181 organizations. In contrast to the self-negating declaration of the Mutual Aid Society ("rather than blaming others, search oneself, and strive toward self-help, self-ennoblement, and self-advancement"), the platform of the new federation called for the liberation of the worker-farmer class, struggle against capitalism, and the advancement of the welfare and livelihood of the workers and farmers. The federation also resolved to organize new unions, assist the existing unions, and investigate (working and living) conditions of the workers and farmers. It was to destroy all organizations that were contrary to the basic principles of the labor-farmer movement—an allusion to the Korean Farm-Tenants Mutual Aid Society, which was a front organization of a notorious pro-Japanese leader Song Pyŏng-jun. The federation also called for an eight-hour working day and a minimum wage standard. Clearly, the labor movement took a radical turn. This was also reflected in the choice of leadership personnel.

The popularity of the new federation was unmistakable. Soon after the federation was established, those groups that had not sent representatives to the inaugural conference applied for membership, and new organizations were established under the federation's auspices. Within the year, the number of labor and farmer groups belonging to the federation reached 260, with a total membership of 53,000.[19] In other words, the KCP, at the time of its founding, had a reservoir of 53,000 persons from which to recruit its membership. The federation also constituted a channel through which the party's programs could be transmitted.

The establishment of the federation was a momentous event in the history of the Korean nationalist movement as well. While the statements adopted by the federation made no reference to Japanese imperialism, there is no doubt that the delegates at the conference considered the federation a tool for struggling against Japanese rule. The Korean workers and farmers could not be "liberated" in true sense as long as Japanese rule continued. Exclusion of the pro-Japanese Tenants Mutual Aid Society from the conference, and its declaration that organizations opposing the "basic principles" of the labor-farmer movement should be destroyed, clearly attest to the nationalistic sentiment of the conference. It was in the interests of the KCP to take over the leadership of this federation and turn it into an organizational instrument of the party. Even by 1924, more than half of the fifty central executive committee members elected were left-wing intellectuals who later joined the KCP.

While the establishment of a united front with the non-communist nationalists required more time than the establishment of the Labor-Farmer Federation, there were no serious obstacles to attaining it. The fact that the Kuomintang and the Chinese Communist Party formed a united front in 1923 and that the arrangement was working out for the benefit of both sides did not escape the attention of the Korean nationalists. In contrast, persistent hostility between the nationalists and communists within Korea had dissipated the strength of both sides to the advantage of the Japanese rulers. Long before the KCP initiated any concrete action on this subject, right-wing newspapers carried editorials exhorting the need to stop the internecine conflict, and urged those involved in the socialist movement to join the nationalist movement.

The communists also reacted favorably to this call because of intellectual developments among the Japanese communists. Between 1925 and 1926, Fukumoto Kazuo, one of the major left-wing intellectual leaders, launched a campaign for a "change in direction," arguing that the socialists should move toward a total political struggle rather than being narrowly confined to economic struggles of the labor and peasant unions. The change of direction from economic struggle to a more politically conscious mass movement became a battle cry among the Korean communists. By February 1927, a pan-national association by the name of Shinganhoe was established, and received the support of both the nationalists and communists. Various intellectual coteries were dissolved, and earnest efforts were made to foster a united front.

Thus the two tasks designated by the Comintern—work among the labor unions, and formation of a united front with the nationalists—were carried out rather smoothly. But the Korean communists encountered the greatest difficulty with the most elementary tasks, those of strengthening the communist party. This, in turn, affected its operations in other areas of activities.

The principal sources of difficulty for the young radicals were the immaturity of some of their followers and the efficiency of the Japanese police. Since many of the leading elements in the communist movement had accumulated experiences as nationalist or communist activists either in China, Japan, Siberia, or within Korea, and since they had witnessed the efficiency of the Japanese police operating not only within Korea and

Japan but also among the Koreans in exile, they took the necessary precautions to protect their secrets. Meetings were held in clandestine fashion and records and messages were written in codes. Every participant knew the risks involved in divulging secrets, and the leadership took whatever precautions they deemed necessary. Since party members were recruited through personal ties between long-established friends, there was little opportunity—at least in the initial years—for police agents to infiltrate the party ranks. There is no record to indicate that the Japanese police were alerted to the possibility that the KCP might be established in Korea in 1925.

But not all the members were invulnerable. The manner in which the first two communist organizations within Korea were destroyed contrasts sharply with the care and toil involved in establishing them, and illustrates the lack of sophistication among some of the lower-echelon members. Thus the KCP organization established in April 1925 was effectively destroyed by the end of the year because of rowdy behavior of a few drunken "communists." On November 15, members of the Shinman Youth Society in Shinuiju, the city facing the Yalu River, were holding a party at a restaurant to celebrate a wedding. After imbibing freely, some of them wandered downstairs and started a brawl with another partying group that included a Korean lawyer and a Japanese policeman. In the course of the drunken melee, one of the young men pointed at his red cloth armband and shouted that "this has succeeded." It was all the clue needed by the police. The subsequent arrests and searches of the houses of some of the leading members of the Society uncovered a number of documents and materials of the Communist Youth League Central Executive Committee intended for delivery to Shanghai. Pak Hŏn-yŏng, the head of the Committee, and others were arrested in Seoul, and within a short period, the Japanese police acquired complete information regarding the incipient Communist Party. Ultimately, about a hundred persons were arrested and eighty-three convicted.[20]

These arrests placed the entire movement in jeopardy, but some of those escaping the dragnet soon began the task of reconstructing the party. But, because the police were expected to have a fairly complete roster of KCP activists and warrants would have been out for all of the known individuals, it became necessary to recruit a relatively unknown figure to lead the "second KCP." The caliber of the man chosen to head the second executive committee perhaps reveals the kind of straits in which the communists found themselves. Kang Tal-yŏng, the man chosen to be the new secretary in charge of the KCP, had not distinguished himself as an intellectual or a political activist. Born around 1885 (making him about forty years old in 1925), his only known mark of distinction was a brief period of imprisonment in connection with the March uprising in 1919, when thousands of others had suffered a similar fate.[21] After he was released, he had been leading a quiet life as a branch manager of Chosŏn Ilbo (the *Korean Daily*), promoting sales and sporadically sending local news to the head office in Seoul. While the position of branch manager of a major newspaper would have commanded the respect of the townspeople, the manager of a newspaper in a small town could hardly qualify as a national figure. Most likely, he was given the assignment only because he would arouse little suspicion and because he was known as a man of determination and managerial skill.[22] Other officers selected to serve on the new executive committee were also men of lesser caliber than the first committee.

Nevertheless, the second executive committee began to operate in early 1926 and within a few months it succeeded in regrouping some 130 members. It also adopted the party rules, reorganized party branches, and established liaison offices and general bureaus in Manchuria and Japan. The principal aims of the new officers were not in stimulating the uninitiated or agitating for proletarian revolution, but largely to bring already aroused individuals into the existing organizational framework. Had their work not been interrupted by an unforeseen event, they might have been able to expand their ranks significantly.

The downfall of the second KCP was caused by a woman's curiosity. Since April 1926, when Sunjong, the last monarch of the old Korean kingdom, had died, there had been considerable unrest in Korea as a whole. Following tradition, many stores in the main thoroughfare of Seoul were closed, along with many private schools. Thousands of mourners also gathered in front of the old palace, and violence broke out frequently. Strikes also began to spread from schools and factories, and it was rumored that there would be mass demonstrations on the day of the funeral. Considering the fact that the March uprising in 1919 was held in the wake of the death of Sunjong's father, it is natural that the communist leaders would see the funeral of his son as an occasion for staging another large-scale demonstration. The leaders in Seoul contacted Kim Ch'an and others now in exile in Shanghai, who promised funds and smuggled in 5,000 copies of scatter-sheets. Those in Seoul, in turn, had some 50,000 copies of scatter-sheets and leaflets printed and prepared for shipment to various localities, waiting for the funds to arrive from Shanghai. The KCP in Seoul was in financial straits, and lacked funds to send out the leaflets.

These materials aroused the interest of a woman worker who was intimate with the household where the materials were stored, and she took two sheets for herself. These were circulated underground among friends. Coincidentally, the police were looking for a man charged with counterfeiting Chinese currency, and when his house was searched, police came upon a crumpled leaflet in an ashtray. This clue inevitably led to the source, where the remaining 50,000 copies were stored, and eventually to Kang Tal-yŏng and his cohorts. Kang refused to divulge information or provide the key to the secret code of his records and even attempted suicide on a number of occasions, but he confessed when the police broke a part of the code. The police acquired extensive information about the party, and needless to say, the KCP was again demolished. More than 100 members of the party were arrested.[23]

These two chance discoveries of the KCP's organizational activities by the Japanese police had an enormous impact on subsequent movement. The two mass arrests virtually removed the most active left-wing leaders from the scene. The efficient manner in which the police netted the subversives also discouraged the others from venturing into this dangerous arena, and discouraged those who had committed themselves to the cause from taking aggressive actions. The police also acquired full range of information about the recruiting of new members, the conduct of propaganda work, sources of funds, and traffic and communication networks, all of which facilitated better surveillance and intelligence gathering. The police could anticipate every move of would-be communists and infiltrate the ranks of the subversives. Since all the veteran organizers were either in jail or had fled abroad, the newly emerging organizers, with little experience, were obliged to confront the better experienced and better equipped police. This was hardly a situation conducive to a flourishing mass movement.

None of the subsequent attempts to revive the communist movement, therefore, remained unnoticed by the police very long. Thus the remnants of the second KCP, in alliance with some of the more recent returnees from Japan as well as a splinter group of the Seoul Youth Society, revived the party organization in December 1926, but most of the activists were arrested in January 1928. This was known as the "third KCP incident" or the "M-L group incident" because the three-group alliance was known as the Marxist-Leninist group. In February 1928, three weeks after the third KCP leaders were arrested, twelve delegates from various provinces in Korea and those from Japan and Manchuria held a meeting to establish the fourth executive committee, but by August of the same year, some 175 members had been arrested. In December 1927, leaders of the main stream of the Seoul Youth Society organized their own KCP, but it was also demolished in April of the following year.

We have already noted some of the causes for these repeated failures, which included immaturity of the participants, chance happenings, laxity in guarding crucial materials, and lack of funds. If any of these defects had not been present, the communists would not have been crushed so easily or thoroughly. The curious woman, for example, would not have had a chance to take the two sheets of propaganda, had the communists been more thorough in protecting their materials or had they had the money to ship them to their intended destinations. All in all, however, one must acknowledge the effectiveness of the Japanese police—or, to put it another way, the adverse nature of the environment.

If we compare the failure of the Korean communists with the experience of their Chinese and Japanese counterparts at similar stages of development, the importance of police effectiveness can be properly understood. Since the momentum of growth was broken by Chiang Kai-shek's coup of 1927, the Chinese Communist Party (CCP) was totally ineffective in the urban areas that were under Kuomintang control. Even though the CCP had attracted a substantial number of urban workers in its heyday after the May Thirtieth incident of 1925, the CCP found the Kuomintang police in the cities simply too formidable. The urban workers did not respond to the CCP's call to revolt against the Kuomintang or to the call for a proletarian revolution. Only by concentrating on the Kiangsi Soviet, in the remote mountains inaccessible to the government forces, was the CCP able to rebuild a nucleus for future growth. The problem for both the Korean and Japanese communists was that their countries were too small in physical size for them to find a safe retreat from which to organize a peasant army or engage in a Long March.

The Japanese communists also shared the same problem of police suppression. In spite of their earnest efforts, the Japanese communists could make no headway because of the police. As soon as they created an organizational structure and began to take action, a police dragnet was cast over the entire group. Thus the first Japanese Communist Party (JCP) was established in July 1922 and demolished in May 1923. The second JCP, organized in December 1926, suffered the same fate in March 1928, when some 1,200 persons were arrested. The party that was reconstructed in November 1928 was demolished between March and June of 1929. The same sequence was repeated year after year.

Facing such a formidable foe, one wonders whether all the other problems which plagued the Korean communists, such as that of factionalism, had any real significance. The most fundamental question that deserved thorough examination was whether the Korean communists should, indeed, establish a formal party structure in Korea; but they were not allowed to debate the question. After receiving the first blow from the police, some of the Japanese communists argued in the spring of 1924 that conditions in Japan were not ripe for the establishment of a communist party. They believed that the existence of an illegal party hampered the more urgent work of laying the foundations for the party by concentrating on the development of unions, peasant associations, Marxist student organizations, and similar groups. But such a position was unacceptable to the Comintern. When a small group of Japanese communists went to the Shanghai Bureau of the Comintern in January 1925, they were severely rebuked by its chief, G. Voitinsky, and ordered to reestablish the party as quickly as possible. To abandon "the only true party of the proletarian masses," even for tactical reasons, was completely unacceptable to the men in Moscow and Shanghai.[24] Aside from the fact that such an action would have raised some complicated theoretical questions related to the role of the proletarian party, the absence of party would have raised problems in command structure and communication. Perhaps the leaders of the fourth KCP had this episode in mind when they resigned from their posts in July 1928. Instead of calling for a dissolution of the party, they requested the Comintern to entrust the task of party reorganization to a communist in Shanghai. For them to continue operating as an executive committee would merely guarantee swift arrest without any conceivable advantage being gained. As we have seen, these leaders were arrested soon after.

The Comintern leaders obviously had reasons to be disappointed, and they issued the December (1928) Theses, a major document on Korea, analyzing the causes of past failures and setting forth future strategies. In brief, the Comintern blamed the past failures on the socio-economic character of the party members and the preponderance of factionalism among them. "The ranks of the Communist Party of Korea have in the past consisted almost exclusively of intellectuals and students. A Communist Party built on such foundations cannot be a consistently Bolshevik and organizationally sound Party," according to the theses.[25] Factionalism, on the other hand, had made the party vulnerable to spies and agent provocateurs, made impossible the necessary organizational foundations for work among the masses, and violated all Marxist norms. The time had come to conduct an all-out attack upon factionalism; to discard the "pseudo-scientific phrases" that had previously dominated the party and develop cadres having genuine communist conceptions and truly scientific Marxist-Leninist modes of thought; and to change the socio-economic character of the party. The Korean communists were told to do their utmost to attract, first of all, industrial workers, and also poor peasants, and to direct their efforts to carrying out an "agrarian revolution." "Only by bringing the peasants under their influence, only by appealing to them by means of intelligible and popular slogans and demands, will the working class and its vanguard be able to accomplish a victorious revolution in Korea."[26] As to the united front, the Korean communists were told first to strengthen the proletarian revolutionary movement and guarantee its complete independence with respect to the petty bourgeois national revolutionary movement; and then to capture that national-revolutionary movement, dissociating it from "compromising national reformism by fighting energetically against all bourgeois-nationalists."

There is no doubt that the Comintern criticisms accurately reflected the facts involved. Of the eighty-three arrested and convicted in the first and second KCP incidents thirty-nine, or 47 percent, were reporters, students, writers, and teachers. Of the additional sixteen placed in the "unemployed" category, many were probably of the same character. Factionalism was also very strong among these men, a tendency shared by intellectuals and subversive activists everywhere.

But when we consider the origins of these movements and take into account the fact that successive "parties" were allowed to exist only briefly before the Japanese police netted them, these were inevitable characteristics of the early years of the Korean communist movement. The simple fact is that the Korean Communist Party had not planted its roots very deeply before it was uprooted by the Japanese police.

Chapter 3

The Social Basis for an Agrarian Revolution

How realistic was the Comintern in ordering the Korean communists to aim at an agrarian revolution? What was the condition of the farmers in Korea? Would they have been susceptible to communist propaganda and organization? Were the Korean communists able to implement these directives?

The Comintern's instruction on agrarian revolution is of particular interest because of the success of the Chinese Revolution based on a peasant army. It is also noteworthy that the Japanese peasants, whose economic conditions resembled in many ways those of their Korean counterparts, became the backbone of Japanese militarism in the 1930s and 1940s rather than serving the cause of a communist revolution. Let us therefore examine the socio-economic conditions in Korea and their effects on communist activities.

The analysis and logic of the Comintern in its December Theses were basically sound. The theses argued that the role of Korea in the system of Japanese imperialism was to be an agrarian hinterland supplying raw material to Japan and serving as a market for Japanese goods; the principal mission of Korea was to supply the Japanese market with rice. The Korean population was fed on inferior food while rice was exported to Japan. The mining resources of the country were used during the World War more intensely, but the industry had barely emerged from its postwar crisis. Korea was a typical colonial country.

The theses also argued correctly that agricultural relations in Korea were chiefly of a pre-capitalist type. The peasants tilled minuscule plots. At the same time, "64.4 percent of all irrigated rice fields and 57.4 percent of all dry fields were cultivated by tenants. A relatively small group of landlords exploited the vast majority of starving peasants. Terrific exploitation makes for the majority of the peasants even simple reproduction of values and labor power impossible."[1]

The Comintern's 1928 analysis can be supported by socio-economic data that have become available since then. Table 1 shows, for example, that per capita consumption of rice, the staple food of the Korean people, decreased substantially as a result of the Japanese policy to use Korea as a source of food supply for Japan. This was in spite of the fact that the area under cultivation increased by 89 percent between 1910 and 1932.[2] As more and more rice was exported to Japan, the Koreans had less and less rice to consume. While the Japanese government did import other grains, such as millet, beans, and corn, from Manchuria to substitute for rice export, the total grain consumption fell far short of the 1910 norm. The farmers also became increasingly impoverished under Japanese rule, as can be seen from the increase in the number and proportion of the tenant farmers and the decrease in owner-cultivators or independent farmers. Many of those who had owned some land of their own but had to rent more land from others to supplant their income sold off their land and became pure tenants. This is shown in Table 2.

The number of landlords and the area they held and placed under tenancy increased because their investment produced lucrative returns. A study conducted by the Japanese indicated that the net profit of investment in an average farm was 7.7 percent in 1931, 8.8 percent in 1932 and 8.5 percent in 1933,[3] when returns from the stock market did not exceed 6 percent (1937 figure).[4] Also, a later study (1937) indicated that the profit from Korean farms was much higher than could be made on the same investment in Japan. While the Japanese farms produced 5.5 percent profit from the rice fields and 4.9 percent from the dry fields, Korean farms produced 8.5 percent and 8.0 percent respectively.[5] As indicated in Table 3, more Japanese capitalists moved into Korea to become landlords, pushing out their Korean counterparts. The influx of Japanese capital and the establishment of the "modern" system of ownership turned the farm lands into simple profit-making enterprises, eradicating the nebulous but more benevolent patron-client relationship that had existed between landlords and tenants in the previous era.[6] In short, Japanese capital dehumanized Korean rural society. All in all, the condition of the Korean farmers was much worse than that of the Japanese farmers. This is reflected in the larger percentage of tenant farmers in Korea as well as the smaller yield per area unit. These can be seen from Tables 4 and 5.

While the landlords found their investments producing favorable returns, the tenant farmers, whose ranks swelled year after year, maintained a precarious existence. The rent paid to the landlords was exorbitant. While there were five common forms of rent in Korea—three under which the tenant paid with the produce of the rented land or with its substitute, and two under which he paid in cash—most of the tenants paid in kind. The three forms of rents in kind were (1) fixed rent, where the tenant surrendered a previously agreed amount from his crop; (2) a rent fixed after the harvest; and (3) rent in which a previously agreed share of the harvest was paid. The practice varied from region to region. The fixed rent was prevalent in two provinces, the "after-harvest" rent was prevalent in three, and share rent was prevalent in nine.[7] The ratio of crop surrendered to the landlords also varied from region to region and according to the kinds of agreements, but in general, the rent was high. The average rate of rent is presented in Table 6.

The average tenant farmer paid 50 to 60 percent of his harvest to the landlord. This did not mean, however, that the tenant was allowed to keep the remainder for himself. According to a governmental study conducted in 1930, 46 to 48 percent of the tenants were required to pay the taxes and other imposts, although government regulations stipulated that the landlord should pay them.[8] In addition to the land taxes, the tenant paid the Irrigation Union for water; he delivered the grain to the landlord, which often involved considerable labor and expense; he paid fees for the inspection of rice; he supplied animal power, seeds, and fertilizers; and he made presents to the landlord. Moreover, most of the landlords were absentee owners and compelled tenants to bring them presents, and to work for them. As a result of all this, tenants were left with only a small portion of their crop. According to one study conducted by a Westerner in Taegu in the early 1920s, the actual net share of the tenant was 17 percent of the crop. Another study made by a Japanese in 1940 in Kangwon province indicated the tenant was left with only 18 percent of the crop.[9]

Considering the minuscule scale of farms and given the low yield per acre of land, many farmers simply could not subsist under such a system. This can be seen from Table 7, in which the income and expenses of farmers in 1924 are shown by classes. In that year, the poorest of the partial tenants and most of the tenant farmers had a deficit. Undoubtedly this situation grew worse after 1924. This resulted in farmers leaving their farms in search of other modes of living, as is shown in Table 8.

These conditions, on the other hand, forced many farmers to abandon their homeland and seek livelihood elsewhere. The two principal countries to which the desperate Korean farmers migrated were Japan and the Chientao region in Manchuria, just across the Tumen River on the eastern part of the Sino-Korean border. While only misery awaited the new immigrants in both places, the displaced found no alternative. Since farms in Japan were already overpopulated and since the dispossessed farmers had no technical skills to offer, the new arrivals could seek only the most demeaning and lowest-paid jobs in the overcrowded Japanese labor market. Because the new arrivals exacerbated the already serious labor problem in Japan, the authorities placed severe restrictions on Korean immigration after 1925;[10] but as shown in Table 9, the number of Koreans in Japan rapidly increased. The situation in Chientao and other parts of Manchuria was hardly more promising. The farm lands there were also overpopulated, and the new arrivals could not hope for anything more than the worst sharecropper arrangement. But survival was at stake, and the number of immigrants increased year by year, as shown in Tables 10 and 11.

While the exodus of these dispossessed farmers undoubtedly reduced the pressure in rural Korea, considerable tension remained. This can be seen from the increasing number of disputes between landlords and tenants. Farmers' unions began to be organized in the early 1920s, and the establishment of the Singanhoe, the pan-national "party," accelerated the pace of organizational movement, as can be seen from Table 12. While the exact role played by these unions cannot be determined, the frequency of peasant strikes increased, as shown in Table 13.

These data leave no room to doubt that the majority of farmers, particularly the tenant farmers who constituted over half of the farm population, had much to complain about. Their condition was such that they were frequently mobilized for collective action.

But the peasants clearly needed leadership to emerge as a revolutionary force. As an astute scholar of the Chinese rural scene remarked on the Chinese peasants, "One simple desire—the will to live—governed their actions and reactions; one remitting task, cultivating the soil in order to keep alive, engaged their attention and energies."[11] Only when persons who were not ordinary peasants provided leadership, were the peasants aroused to action. It should be added, however, that both the Chinese and Korean peasants were very volatile. Professor Hsiao noted that the Chinese peasants were "habitually ready to accept leadership offered by persons with economic status different than their own."[12] Considering the economic conditions of the Korean farmers and reflecting upon the experience of the farmers during the Tonghak Rebellion that swept the country in the 1890s, one is inclined to draw similar conclusions about the Korean farmers.

A comment by a Japanese author of a massive study of Korean agriculture, Kobayakawa Kurō, is worthy of note in this connection:

> Traditionally, the position of the tenants in Korea has been weak and they rarely displayed any resistance against the tyranny of the landlords and their agents. Their (recent) expression of self-interest can, of course, be attributed to the change of times, but it is more complicated. In the opinion of this author, while organizational movements described above have been affected by the currents of time and the influence of the labor movement in the cities, it is very doubtful that the members of these organizations acted on the basis of much self-awareness. These organized movements were not much more than those of the leaders; a superficial phenomenon.[13]

In the opinion of Kobayakawa, the farmers wished no more than gradual improvement of their lots, but the leaders of various movements tried to link the desires of the farmers with radical movements that called for the sudden destruction of old customs and the establishment of a new world. Kobayakawa felt that the tenant farmers were not immersed in these ideas, and that they simply followed the leaders blindly. This, according to Kobayakawa, was why the movement did not fulfill the expectations of the leaders, in spite of good prospects.[14] But the Japanese government found the situation grave enough to launch a thorough study of the tenancy situation in 1927, issued special instructions to provincial governors to resolve conflicts between the landlords and tenants, and in 1929, appointed high ranking Tenant Officers

(Kosaku-kan) in various provinces to prevent or mediate tenancy disputes.[15] These actions were tantamount to a declaration of war against the organizers of the tenant farmers. The odds were, of course, clearly in favor of the authorities. They not only had the power to oversee, mediate, or control the peasantry but also had the power to arrest and imprison all "troublemakers" that opposed government policies.

The basic problem for the communist organizers remained the same as before—the efficiency of the Japanese police. No sooner did communist cadres arrive from China and the Soviet Union, than they were detected and arrested. Soon after the December Theses were issued, a small number of Korean communists remaining in Manchuria dispatched agents into Korea under the direction of the Chinese Communist Party, which had been given command over the Korean communists in Chinese territory. Other communists in Shanghai and Peking did the same, but they fared no better. All the agents could do was to organize small coteries of students and workers in industrial centers, and then mimeograph and distribute leaflets until they were rounded up. The Comintern and Profintern, operating through their branches in Khvarovsk and Vladivostok, sent in their agents (one in 1930, two in 1931, seven in 1932, and so on), but their results were equally unspectacular. They organized some workers, mimeographed and distributed pamphlets, and infiltrated the existing legal unions, and so on, but they were all rounded up within a year of their arrival. Often, the distribution of mimeographed materials became the cue for police arrest. While the agents were specifically instructed to "publish leaflets, factory papers, popular pamphlets, posters, etc." to throw light on the life of the workers, and to give form to the demands and leadership to the class struggle of the Korean proletariat,[16] the Japanese police were ever alert to those tell-tale signs. Table 14 shows the number of communist cases "broken" by the police and the number of individuals implicated. While the total number of persons arrested for the crime of attempting to "change the polity (kokutai) or to deny the private property system" was fairly large, the average number of persons implicated in a case shows the difficulty of organizing a mass movement.

While the agents from China and the Soviet Union did not make much progress either in the factories or on the farms, some of those who might be labeled indigenous local leaders achieved rather impressive results among the peasants in the North and South Hamgyŏng provinces in the northeastern corner of the Korean peninsula. Some of these men planted such a deep root among the peasants in this region between 1930 and 1937 that the Japanese police called this the worst affected area. Almost every prefecture (*kun*) in the triangular area of Unggi in the northeast, Hyesan in the northwest, and Wonsan in the south was affected by communist movement at one time or another. The mobilized peasants were tenacious and ferocious in pursuing their goals. Many of the organized movements were detected and the participants arrested by the police, but many others emerged in turn, so that the Japanese police were not able to completely eradicate the influence of the communists. They clearly established a mood of defiance among the local peasantry against Japanese rule and the wealthy landlords.

It will be sufficient here to note a few examples of organizational activities among the peasants. In each case, one can see the strong impact of the initial leadership. One also finds that the most vigorous leadership was provided by professional revolutionaries rather than by those who worked with hoes or plows.

One of these leaders was Yi Mun-hong, a veteran communist of M.L. group origin, who had been active among the Korean communists in Manchuria since 1927. He is credited with having organized red farmers' unions in Munch'ŏn, Kowŏn, and Yŏnghŭng, all in between Wonsan and Hamhŭng. Yi's efforts since August 1931 were directed toward the reorganization of the already existing farmers' unions into red tenants' unions. In Munch'ŏn, he won the support of the chairman and other leaders of the existing Farmers' Union to establish reading circles at the *ri* level (cluster of villages), and to publish an organ. Some of the participants were arrested in December of the same year, but the red tenants' union was reconstructed in February 1932, only to suffer another wave of arrests in May. In June of 1933, when Yi was already in jail, the union was reconstructed by peasants and continued the organizational and propaganda activities until June 1934 when the police rounded up most of the participants. In the meantime, Yi also directed his efforts to organizing the workers in Hŭngnam. Sometime in 1932, however, Yi was arrested along with some 100 members of the Chemical Workers' Union in Hŭngnam.[17]

The movement in Hongwon followed the same pattern. The Hongwon Farmers' Union had been established in December 1927 with the approval of the government by some thirty individuals. The two prominent leaders were Ŏm Won-sik and Chŏng Ryŏm-su, both local residents. Ŏm was a schoolteacher who had been to Seoul with hopes for higher education but had failed. Chŏng had been to Japan and attended Nippon College for seven months before he was obliged to return home for reasons of health and funds. Both of them read Marxist literature and held a strong desire for Korean independence, and were in sympathy with communism. Under their leadership, the Union expanded in influence and a number of local branches were established. By early 1931, the Farmers' Union emerged as the most powerful Korean organization in the prefecture.

Gradually the union turned to mass actions and violence. In May 1931, for example, approximately 1,000 farmers from various parts of the prefecture gathered in front of the prefectural government office in Hongwon to petition for the deferment of the household tax. This movement attracted another 1,000 persons attending the periodic market in town. Only the armed police were able to disperse the crowd and prevent a riot.

Between August and September 1931, the members of the union turned to violence. Leaders of one of the local branches decided to annul all debts incurred by the peasants at usurious rates by eliminating all credit documents. Between August 29 and September 21, organized groups of farmers invaded the homes of scores of creditors, forcibly collected credit documents, and burned them to ashes. The police, of course, took immediate action against the radicals, arresting 250 persons and outlawing the Farmers' Union.[18] Several individuals attempted to revive the organization in late 1931 and early 1932, but the police arrested them before any progress had been made.[19]

The seed for the most obstinate and ferocious organizational activities among the farmers, however, was implanted by Hyŏn Ch'un-bong, a graduate of the Communist University in Moscow who had served briefly as a cadre of the KCP branch in Manchuria in 1927. Evidently he made careful plans for his future activities while he was in prison between December 1928 and August 1932. He proceeded to organize a movement as soon as he was released, recruiting comrades from Unggi, Najin, Ch'ŏngjin, Kyŏngsŏng, and Sŏngjin. On the occasion of the anniversary of the October Revolution (November 4) in 1934, his groups produced 12,000 copies of leaflets and scattered them in the streets and alleys of all these cities and towns. This act, however led to the arrest of sixty-four members of his group.

In contrast to his failure in activities directed toward the urban workers, his efforts among the farmers in Myŏngch'ŏn and Kilchu yielded significant results. In April 1934, he launched the Farmers' Union Movement Myŏngch'ŏn Left-wing (Nongmin Chohap Undong Myŏngch'ŏn Chwa-ik), which quickly expanded. The police arrested 213 persons in January 1935, only eight months after the organizational movement began.

The arrests, however, did not destroy the movement. In May 1935, three local farmers reconstructed the movement, establishing cells, local committees, and reading circles. They also organized debate meetings and lectures to indoctrinate the farmers. The new prefectural headquarters also mimeographed various organs, propaganda materials, and leaflets. In October, it even published theses on the "Combat Duties of the Farmers' Union Myŏngch'ŏn Left-wing," calling for expansion and consolidation of the revolutionary farmers' union. The members were urged to forge themselves with ironlike discipline and engage in fierce struggle against the enemy and resist white terrorism.

The use of violence became an accepted mode of operation of the Myŏngch'ŏn group. Having suffered a grave blow from the police on a previous occasion, it was decided that the union members should not peacefully surrender to the police. The members were instructed to carry sticks, knives, or sickles to resist the police, and if one member were arrested other members were to rescue him forcibly. Large numbers of sticks, sickles, and clubs were stored in strategic locations. These exhortations evidently had the desired effect. In one incident, a union member resisting arrest attempted to wrest away a pistol from the arresting police officer, who shot the man to death. In four cases, large numbers of farmers assaulted police stations to rescue the arrested persons, succeeding on two occasions.

The Myŏngch'ŏn Union members also took other measures to protect themselves. Eighteen boys from eleven to sixteen years of age were assigned the tasks of spying on the police stations. Informers were planted in the government sponsored Self-Defense Corps. On fourteen occasions, the union members physically assaulted government spies and others designated as reactionaries, not only to punish the enemies but to intimidate others. The group also constructed underground hideouts and used caves for meetings and for printing propaganda materials. The police eventually discovered thirty-five such hideouts, which were protected by rings of warning systems. The group also had stored grains and fruits in these hideouts for prolonged confrontation. The needs for the movement were met not only by voluntary contributions but by robbery and theft.

There is no doubt that this radical movement received widespread support from the local peasantry. The police began the round-up of union members in December 1935 and completed the operation in August 1936, but when all the known members were arrested, the number reached 1,043. The police also learned that there were 176 cells, 48 committees, and 4 local union branches. In addition, there were 23 cells among the fishermen, 7 fishermen's committees, and 2 fishermen's unions.[20] These arrests did not end the movement. The police authorities declared the end of the movement in Myŏngch'ŏn only in November 1937, after arresting another 228 persons between September and November.[21] The movement in the neighboring prefecture of Kilchu, which was also under the direction of Hyŏn Ch'un-bong and shared similar characteristics with the movement in Myŏngch'ŏn, produced another 200 to 300 arrests.[22]

Thus the Hamgyŏng provinces displayed a strong potential for an agrarian revolution called for by the Comintern. Those farmers who had been mobilized for the burning of credit documents and other violent acts could easily have been mobilized for other more revolutionary activities, such as armed struggle against the Japanese colonial regime. Why was it that the peasant movement in the Hamgyŏng provinces was more successful than in other provinces? How should we assess the significance of these victories?

The Japanese police authorities analyzing the situation in 1937 attributed the extraordinarily strong and violent movements in the Hamgyŏng provinces to the following factors: (1) the generally ferocious character of the residents of the area; (2) strong national consciousness; (3) influence of the March First Movement of 1919; (4) propaganda and instigation by students who had studied outside of the area; (5) the influence of social organizations; and (6) the communist emphasis on Hamgyŏng provinces as the target area.[23] This analysis, however, leaves much to be desired. With the exception of factors (1) and (6), the same could have been said about a few other regions of Korea. Had the communists selected another region as the target, would they have reaped the same results? Does the ferocity or unruly character of the people in the Hamgyŏng provinces alone explain the unique success of the communist organizers? One clearly must seek other explanations.

Economic factors, however, do not explain the successes. The ratio of tenant farmers in these provinces was about half the national average.[24] Tenant fees or rents were also below the national average,[25] and so was

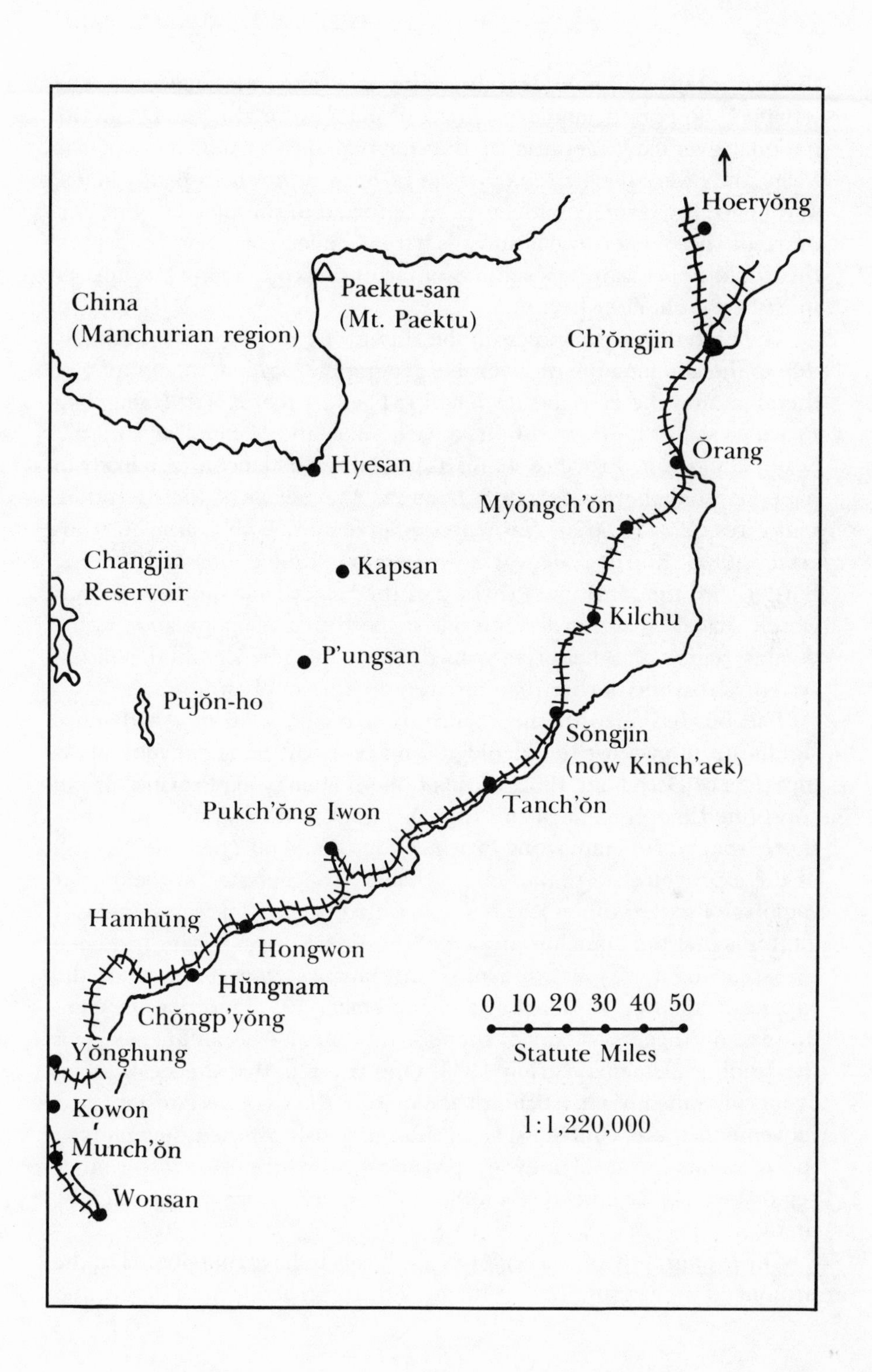
Hoeryŏng
Paektu-san
(Mt. Paektu)
China
(Manchurian region)
Ch'ŏngjin
Ŏrang
Hyesan
Myŏngch'ŏn
Changjin
Reservoir
Kapsan
Kilchu
P'ungsan
Pujŏn-ho
Sŏngjin
(now Kinch'aek)
Tanch'ŏn
Pukch'ŏng Iwon
Hamhŭng
Hongwon
Hŭngnam
0 10 20 30 40 50
Chŏngp'yŏng
Statute Miles
Yŏnghung
Kowon
1:1,220,000
Munch'ŏn
Wonsan

the percentage of landlords transferring taxes and other burdens to the tenants.[26] Reported landlord-tenant disputes were also far below the national average.[27] Because of the mountainous terrain, most of the farm lands were devoted to dry-field farming rather than paddy fields, and hence the farmers in the area were forced to consume less rice and more of the coarser grains such as barley, millet, corn, and beans, but this could not constitute a significant factor of explanation. The answer must be sought elsewhere.

The high degree of success in the Hamgyŏng provinces was probably due to the combination of favorable geographic location, topography of the area, and the effective leadership. The fact that North Hamgyŏng Province shares borders with the Soviet Union and Manchuria, and that South Hamgyŏng Province shares its borders with Manchuria, is likely to have affected the residents of the area. As a result of their location, many residents of these provinces migrated to both countries, thus establishing informal networks of communication and traffic. The border with the Maritime Province of the Soviet Union, of course, was closely sealed by both sides, but one suspects that the population in the border region was better informed about the ideology and political system across the border than an average Korean elsewhere.

The borderline with the Manchurian region of China had more significant impact for the ideological make-up of the Hamgyŏng provinces. As of December 1932, those of South Hamgyŏng Province origin constituted 9.4 percent of the Korean population in Manchuria, while those from North Hamgyŏng Province constituted 60.2 percent.[28] Those of these provinces were particularly heavily concentrated in the border region along the Tumen River, as one would expect. The significance of all this is that the Manchurian side of the Sino-Korean border had been the scene of a very active armed anti-Japanese movement since the Japanese takeover of Manchuria in September 1931, and that the communist contingents—many of them being Korean—began to emerge as the leading elements during 1933. One suspects that the news about events in Manchuria, particularly the news of the vigorous anti-Japanese movements there, consciously and subconsciously affected the minds of the residents in the Hamgyŏng provinces, while the Koreans in other regions would have been less well-informed and hence less affected by them.

The topography of the region is also likely to have contributed to the prolonged underground movements. The construction of underground hideouts and the use of caves was suited to the rugged topography. Except for the small coastal plains near Wonsan and Hamhŭng, these two provinces were mostly mountainous, and this is likely to have hindered the search and seizure of activists by the police, thus prolonging the movements.

Credit must also be given to the leadership. Certain individuals were more gifted than others in arousing, mobilizing, and leading the farmers. The failure of many an agent from the Soviet Union and China, who had received years of intensive training there, indicates the difficulty of imparting organizational skills at the grassroots level. The task of expanding the organization without being detected by the police required extraordinary acumen, daring, and luck. One must say that very few individuals were endowed with these qualities.

The odds against these leaders, however, were enormous. Case after case of arrest leaves no doubt of the efficiency of the police system. The Japanese state, on the other hand, possessed a firm determination to eradicate subversive elements and had almost limitless resources to pursue its goal. As early as May 1931, when the communist organizers began to be active, the government increased the number of police personnel in the region.[29] In 1936, when the government decided that the situation in the region called for much more than simple suppressive measures, it launched a massive effort at "thought purification," promising amnesty to surrendered activists, providing economic aid to appropriate individuals, organizing the young men into "self-defense corps" to indoctrinate and control them, and carrying out massive lecture campaigns.[30] The Japanese had acquired considerable experience in counterinsurgency activities in Manchuria against the Chinese and Korean communists there, and the government was prepared to use any measure necessary to eliminate the communists.

Given the topography and geographic location of this region, as well as the strain of radicalism and violent tendencies among the farmers, one might be tempted to ask whether they should not have organized "revolutionary bases" in the remote mountains and engaged in guerrilla activities. But any attempt to organize such a base would have been foredoomed. The East Manchuria Special Committee of the Chinese Communist Party did indeed organize "soviets" in Yenchi, Wangch'ing, and Hunch'un prefectures across the Tumen River between 1932 and 1933, but all six of them were soon destroyed because of a lack of mass support, a lack of food, and the intensive assault of the Japanese forces.[31]

It should be added also that the only way the farmers in Korea could obtain firearms was by attacking and taking them from the Japanese police and the army. The Japanese authorities had absolute control over all firearms, and the private sale of them was simply unknown.

Thus an agrarian revolution and the overthrow of Japanese imperialism were closely linked. Without a political revolution, it was simply impossible to bring about an agrarian revolution. The Comintern obviously recognized this when it stated in the December Theses: "Thus the overthrow of imperialism and the revolutionary solution of the agrarian problem is the main objective historical meaning of the revolution in Korea in the first phases of its development. In this sense the Korean Revolution will be a bourgeois-democratic revolution."[32]

The Comintern, however, departed from this line of argument when it reversed the order of these two revolutions. Rather than placing priority on anti-imperialist political revolution and recognizing its own analysis that the revolution in Korea should be a bourgeois-democratic revolution, the leaders in Moscow let the events in China and elsewhere influence their analysis of the situation in Korea as well as their strategies toward it. As is well-known, the Chinese communists suffered a major disaster in 1927 when Chiang Kai-shek turned against them and virtually annihilated them. This is probably why the Comintern noted in the December Theses, the "rapprochement of Japanese imperialism and the big native landowners" and its certain effect on "the position of a considerable section of the intelligentsia which plays a big role in the organization and leadership of the nationalist movement." The Korean communists were to "expect growing national reformist tendencies in their ranks, a diminishing of their revolutionary character, and their transformation into a loyal opposition." Therefore, the Comintern decided that "a victory over the imperialist yoke *presupposes* a revolutionary solution of the agrarian problem and the establishment of a democratic dictatorship of the proletariat and the peasants (in the form of Soviets) through which the bourgeois-democratic revolution under the hegemony of the proletariat is transformed into a Socialist Revolution." (Emphasis added.)[33] Through such rather dubious reasoning, the Comintern decided not only to reject the big landowners but also the national bourgeoisie and the intelligentsia. The Korean revolution was to be undertaken by the meager force of the proletariat in alliance with the peasantry.

The radical tendency of the Comintern intensified in the succeeding years. In September 1930, the Profintern (the Red International of

Labor Unions, a Comintern subsidiary organization) instructed the Korean communists to "ruthlessly expose" the reactionary character of the Korean General Confederation of Labor, a "reformist" body whose 45,000 members were headed by "petty bourgeois and nationalist elements," as well as the Shinganhoe, a united front organization, which was characterized as a "national reformist organization."[34] Soon the Korean communists echoed the argument, and by mustering all of their strength, they dissolved the Shinganhoe at its second national convention in May 1931. The Japanese authorities, who had prohibited the Shinganhoe from holding annual conventions on two previous years, presented no obstacles. They had already decided that the Shinganhoe was becoming too powerful as an instrument of Korean resistance against the Japanese rule.[35] The Japanese cause would be better served by splitting the nationalists and communists. While the nationalist leaders objected strenuously against the dissolution of the Shinganhoe, they were powerless before this joint maneuver of the communists and the Japanese authorities. The police did not even permit the nationalist opposition to issue a statement after the national convention passed the resolution to dissolve itself.

The radical and violent activities of the peasants described in this chapter took place in this context. The question that remains to be asked is whether the Comintern's radical line and the equally radical actions of the Korean communists indeed advanced the cause of either the anti-imperialist revolution or the agrarian revolution. It must be said that whatever victories local leaders achieved from time to time, they were all ephemeral. An occasional burst of violence may have released the frustration of the farmers and satisfied their pride, but it inevitably invited government suppression. Meanwhile the ranks of the revolutionaries were badly depleted.

The Comintern's radicalism also weakened the nationalist camp, which was left with no organization to anchor its movement. When the Comintern decided at its Seventh Congress in 1935 that it needed the support of all anti-Fascist elements everywhere, including the bourgeoisie and the intelligentsia, it could find neither a communist nor a nationalist organization within Korea that could be useful to the Comintern. Considering the fact that the Japanese authorities abolished the two leading Korean language newspapers in Korea, *Tong-a Ilbo* and *Chosŏn Ilbo*, in August 1940, the days of the Shinganhoe would have been numbered even if the communists had not spearheaded the dissolution movement. But had the Shinganhoe been allowed to exist a few more years after 1931, it could have strengthened the anti-Japanese movement in general and laid a stronger foundation for the popular anti-Fascist front demanded by the Comintern. Thus the Comintern's radicalism not only inflicted immediate damage on the Korean communist movement but also stifled the Korean people's long-range struggle against Japan.

TABLE 1

EXPORT, IMPORT, AND DOMESTIC CONSUMPTION OF RICE IN KOREA, 1910–1938

Year	Total Production[a]	Index	Export[a]	Index	Percentage of Export	Import[a]	Net Domestic Consumption[a]	Population[b]	Per Capita Consumption in sŏk	Index
1910	10,405	100	544	100	5.2	13	9,874	14,055	0.705	100
1914	14,130	136	2,559	470	18.1	31	11,602	16,278	0.712	101
1919	12,708	122	2,090	369	16.5	56	10,674	17,288	0.617	88
1924	13,219	127	4,758	875	36.0	970	9,431	19,015	0.496	70
1929	13,701	132	5,433	999	39.7	585	8,853	20,256	0.437	62
1930	19,180	184	8,412	1,554	43.8	66	10,834	20,262	0.535	76
1931	15,872	153	7,585	1,376	47.8	105	8,392	20,599	0.407	58
1932	16,345	157	8,074	1,484	49.4	110	8,381	20,791	0.403	57
1933	18,192	175	9,501	1,746	55.2	124	8,815	21,125	0.417	59
1934	16,717	161	9,001	1,654	53.9	292	7,872	21,891	0.359	51
1935	17,884	172	9,573	1,759	53.5	156	8,467	22,047	0.384	54
1936	19,410	187	7,201	1,324	37.1	199	12,408	22,355	0.555	79
1937	26,796	258	10,996	2,021	41.0	44	15,844	22,633	0.701	99
1938	24,138	232	6,894	1,267	28.7	308	17,552	22,800	0.769	109

SOURCE: Kim Yong-gi, *Chosŏn ui nongŏp* (Agriculture in Korea), Seoul, 1946), p. 6

[a] Unit: in 1000 sŏk. One sŏk is 4.96 bushels.

[b] Unit: 1,000.

TABLE 2

FARM FAMILIES BY ECONOMIC CLASSES, 1914–1932

Year	Absentee Landlords (A)	Farming Landlords (B)	Percent (A+B)	Farmer Owners	Percent	Farmer-owner -partial Tenants	Percent	Tenants	Percent	Burnt-field Farmers	Percent	Total
A. FARM FAMILIES												
1914	46,754		1.8	569,517	22.0	1,065,705	41.1	911,261	35.1	—	—	2,593,237
1919	16,274	74,112	3.4	525,830	19.7	1,045,606	39.3	1,003,003	37.6	—	—	2,664,825
1920	15,565	75,365	3.3	529,177	19.5	1,017,780	37.4	1,082,742	39.8	—	—	2,720,819
1923	17,904	82,498	3.7	527,494	19.5	951,667	35.2	1,123,275	41.6	—	—	2,702,838
1926	20,571	84,043	3.8	525,747	19.1	895,721	32.5	1,193,099	43.3	—	—	2,753,497
1929	21,326	83,170	3.7	507,384	18.0	885,594	31.5	1,284,471	45.6	34,332	1.2	2,813,277
1932	32,890	71,933	3.6	476,351	16.2	742,961	25.3	1,546,456	52.8	60,497	2.1	2,931,088
B. INDEX OF FARM FAMILIES												
1914	100			100.0		100.0		100.0		—	—	100.0
1919	194			92.3		98.1		110.1		—	—	102.8
1920	194			92.9		95.5		118.8		—	—	104.9
1923	215			92.6		89.3		123.3		—	—	104.2
1926	224			92.3		84.0		130.9		—	—	106.2
1929	224			89.1		83.1		140.9		100	—	108.5
1932	224			83.6		69.7		169.7		176.2	—	113.0

SOURCE: Suzuki Masafumi, *Chōsen keizai no gendankai* (Present Stage of Korean Economy), (Tokyo, 1938), pp. 437–439. Suzuki provides data for 1914 and consecutively from 1919 to 1936 inclusive. His table is based on *Chōsen no nōgyō* (Agriculture in Korea), (no other data given) published by the Bureau of Agriculture and Forestry of the Korean Government-General.

TABLE 3

LARGE LANDLORDS BY NATIONALITIES (JAPANESE AND KOREAN), 1919–1936

Year	Holding 100 chŏngbo and above[a]			Holding 200 chŏngbo and above	
	Japanese	Korean	Others	Japanese	Korean
1919	321	360	–	169	186
1921	233	389	–	178	67
1923	360	344	–	170	45
1925	361	290	–	192	45
1927	361	340	2	172	40
1929	361	290	2	187	46
1931	361	319	2	187	49
1933	406	308	4	192	43
1936	380	336	4	181	49

SOURCE: In Chŏng-sik, *Chosŏn ui t'oji munje* (The Land Problem in Korea), (Seoul, 1946), p. 92. The author based his calculation on land tax returns.

[a] One chŏngbo, or Chō in Japanese, is 2.45 acres.

TABLE 4

PERCENT OF FARM FAMILIES BY ECONOMIC CLASSES, JAPAN AND KOREA, 1930S

Countries	Farmer-owner	Farmer-owner Partial Tenants	Tenants	Farm Workers
Japan	31	42	27	–
Korea	18	27	51	4

SOURCE: Zenkoku Keizai Chōsa Kikan Rengōkai Chōsen Shibu (Federation of Economic Study Agencies throughout Japan, Korea Branch) (ed.), *Chōsen keizai nempō* (Korean Economic Annual Report), 1941–1942 ed. (Tokyo, 1943), p. 228.

TABLE 5

COMPARISON OF AVERAGE CROP PER TAN IN JAPAN AND KOREA (FIVE-YEAR AVERAGE, 1935–1940), IN KOKU[a]

Countries	Rice	Wheat	Barley	Beans	Millet
Japan	2.056	1.399	2.009	0.699	1.163
Korea	1.355	0.595	0.945	0.479	0.656

SOURCE: *Chōsen Keizai Nempō*, 1941–42 ed., p. 228.

[a] Tan is 0.425 acres; 10 tan constitute a chŏngbo. Koku (or sŏk in Korean) is equivalent to 4.96 bushels.

TABLE 6

SHARE OF HARVEST GOING TO THE LANDLORD, KOREA IN 1930
(PERCENT OF TOTAL HARVEST)

	Fixed Rent	"After-Harvest"	"Share" Rent
A. *Dry Fields*			
Highest	58-90	50-79	50-80
Common	40-51	45-60	50-55
Lowest	20-39	30-44	5-50
B. *Rice Fields*			
Highest	55-80	50-65	47-75
Common	35-50	49-60	40-55
Lowest	3-47	20-43	10-50

SOURCE: Chōsen Nōkai (Agricultural Association of Korea), *Chōsen Nōgyō hattatsu-shi, Seisaku-hen* (History of Agricultural Development in Korea, Policy Part), (Seoul, 1944), pp. 540–542. Based on a Korean Government-General publication of 1933.

For explanation of Fixed Rent, "After-Harvest," and "Share" Rent, see p. 35.

TABLE 7

INCOME AND EXPENSES OF FARMERS IN KOREA, 1924
(UNIT: YEN)

Classes		Big Farmers[a]	Middle Farmers	Small Farmers	Poor Farmers	Average
Farmer-owner	Income	1,237	732	441	314	646
	Expenses	1,004	635	401	297	559
	Net	233	97	40	17	87
Farmer-owner Partial Tenant	Income	1,015	555	381	241	476
	Expenses	924	551[b]	374	242	451
	Net	91	44	7	–1	25
Tenant farmer	Income	824	519[c]	333	215	403
	Expenses	808	596	353	227	414
	Net	16	–5	–20	–12	11
Hired Farm Worker	Income	—	—	—	—	102
	Expenses	—	—	—	—	106
	Net	—	—	—	—	-4

SOURCE: Gunseibu, Komonbu (Division of Advisors, Department of Defense, Manchukuo), *Manshū kyōsanhi no kenkyū* (A Study of Communist Insurgents in Manchuria), n.p., 1937, p. 498. This source cites an untitled report of the Bureau of Home Affairs (Naimu-kyoku) of the Korean Government-General, 1925.

[a]Big farmers are those who till 3 chŏngbo (chō in Japanese) or more; middle farmers, 1 chongbo or more; small farmers, 0.3 chŏngbo or more; poor farmers, below 0.3 chŏngbo. One chŏngbo is 2.45 acres.

[b]Although there are obvious errors in these figures, they are presented as in the original. Probably should be 511.

[c]Probably should be 591.

TABLE 8

NUMBER OF FARMERS LEAVING KOREAN FARMS DURING 1926

Province	Farmers Leaving
Kyŏnggi	2,782
North Chungchŏng	5,897
South Chungchŏng	1,936
North Chŏlla	8,287
South Chŏlla	13,535
North Kyŏngsang	57,055
South Kyŏngsang	31,837
Hwanghae	2,789
South Pyŏngan	5,005
North Pyŏngan	3,369
Kangwŏn	3,200
South Hamgyŏng	12,416
North Hamgyŏng	2,004
Total	150,112

SOURCE: Gunseibu, Komonbu (Division of Advisors, Department of Defense, Manchukuo), *Manshū kyōsanhi no kenkyū* (A Study of Communist Insurgents in Manchuria), n.p., 1937, pp. 506–507. Based on Zenshō Eisuke, *Chōsen no kosaku kanshū* (Tenancy Custom in Korea).

TABLE 9

KOREANS IN JAPAN, 1910–1944

Year End	Number	(Census Data)
1910	250 est.	
1911	1,500 est.	
1912	2,500 est.	
1913	3,635	
1914	3,542	
1915	3,917	
1916	5,624	
1917	14,520	
1918	22,000	
1919	26,605	
1920	30,189	(40,755)
1921	38,651	
1922	59,851	
1923	80,617	
1924	120,238	
1925	133,710	
1926	148,503	
1927	175,911	
1928	243,328	
1929	276,031	
1930	298,091	(419,009)
1936	625,678	
1940	1,190,444	(1,241,315)
1944	1,936,843	

SOURCE: Tsuboe Senji, *Zai Nihon Chōsenjin jōkyō* (The Condition of the Koreans in Japan), (Tokyo, 1965), pp. 9–10.

TABLE 10

POPULATION IN THE CHIENTAO REGION OF MANCHURIA, 1910–1931

Year	Koreans	Index	Chinese	Index
1910	109,500	100	33,500	100
1912	163,000	148	49,000	146
1916	203,426	185	60,896	181
1921	307,806	281	73,748	220
1926	356,016	335	86,347	257
1931	396,847	363	120,394	359

SOURCE: Gunseibu, Komonbu (Division of Advisors, Department of Defense, Manchukuo), *Manshū kyōsanhi no kenkyū* (A Study of Communist Insurgents in Manchuria), n.p. 1937. p. 543.

TABLE 11

KOREANS IN MANCHURIA, 1919–1934

Year	Number	Index
1919	431,198	100.0
1920	459,427	106.5
1921	488,656	113.3
1922	515,865	119.6
1923	528,027	122.5
1924	531,857	123.3
1925	531,973	123.4
1926	542,185	125.7
1927	558,280	129.5
1928	577,052	133.8
1929	597,677	138.6
1930	607,119	140.8
1931	630,982	146.3
1932	672,649	156.0
1933	673,794	156.3
1934	719,988	167.0

SOURCE: Same as Table 10, pp. 508–509.

TABLE 12

KOREAN SOCIO-POLITICAL ORGANIZATIONS, 1920–1930

				Type of Organizations				
Year	Nationalist	Socialist	Labor	Farmer	Youths	Boys	Outcasts	Total
1920	–	11	33	–	251	1	–	296
1921	–	18	90	3	446	14	–	571
1922	–	19	81	23	488	25	–	636
1923	–	55	111	107	584	43	–	900
1924	1	86	91	112	742	81	83	1,196
1925	1	83	128	126	847	127	99	1,411
1926	2	38	182	119	1,092	203	130	1,766
1927	104	85	352	160	1,127	247	150	2,225
1928	182	75	432	307	1,320	293	153	2,762
1929	214	56	465	564	1,433	366	162	3,260
1930	246	56	561	943	1,509	461	165	3,941

SOURCE: Chōsen Sōtokufu, Keimu-kyoku (Police Affairs Bureau, Korean Government-General), *Saikin ni okeru Chōsen chian jōkyō* (Recent conditions of public security in Korea), Seoul, 1934, pp. 168–169.

NOTE: It is believed that "youths" refers to individuals of seventeen years of age or older, and "boys" to those under seventeen.

TABLE 13

TENANT FARMERS' STRIKES, 1920–1939

Year	Number of Strikes			Number of Participants		
	Source 1	Source 2	Source 3	Source 1	Source 2	Source 3
1920	15	15		4,140	4,140	
1921	27	27		2,967	2,967	
1922	24	24		3,539	2,539	
1923	176	176		9,060	9,060	
1924	164	164		6,929	6,929	
1925	11	204		2,646	4,002	
1926	17	198		2,118	2,745	
1927	22	275		3,285	3,973	
1928	30	1,390		3,572	4,863	
1929	36	423		2,620	5,315	
1930	93	726		10,037	12,132	
1931	57	667		5,486	10,282	
1932	51	300		2,909	4,686	
1933	66			2,494		
1934	106			4,113		
1935	71		159	2,795		2,246
1936	56		544	3,462		3,834
1937	24		31	2,234		2,771
1938	30		27	1,338		1,316
1939			24			969

SOURCES: 1. Chōsen Sōtokufu, Keimu-kyoku (Police Affairs Bureau, Korean Government-General), *Saikin ni okeru Chōsen Chian jōkyō*, Seoul, 1934, pp. 156–158, pp. 190–192. 2. Gunseibu, Komonbu (Division of Advisors, Department of Defense, Manchukuo), *Manshū kyōsanhi no kenkyū* (A Study of Communist Insurgents in Manchuria), n.p., 1937, pp. 540–541, based on Korean Government-General, *Chōsa geppō* (Monthly Research Report). 3. Kōtō Hōin, Kenjikyoku (Prosecutors' Bureau, High Court, Korean Government-General), *Shisō ihō* (Thought Report Series), nos. 6, 10, 15, 19, 22.

NOTE: It is interesting that these Japanese government authorities used different sets of data. As can be seen, there is considerable discrepancy between the statistics for 1925 and after. Reasons for this are offered by Yi Yŏ-song and Kim Se-yong in their *Su-cha Chosŏn* (Statistical study of Korea) (Seoul, 1933), IV, 86–87 which also presents a table on the tenant farmers' strikes, 1920–1931. They say that the first set (cited here as source 1) is from statistics collected by the Bureau of Police Affairs of the Korean Government-General and hence includes statistics on only those incidents that invited the attention of the police. The second set (source 2) was collected by the Shoksan-kyoku (Bureau of Development, or Bureau of Increase in Production) and includes almost every incident of a strike or dispute. This bureau did not collect data before 1925, and relied on data collected by the police bureau for the earlier period. Yi and Kim reproduced the figures for the years between 1920 and 1931 in their work, citing *Chosen keisatsu gaiyo* (Synopsis of the Korean Police) for set 1 and *Chosa geppo* (see source 2 of this table), June 1932, for set 2. It should be noted that the Japanese military (the Advisers' Department of the Manchukuo Ministry of Defense), which had access to all information collected by the Korean Government-General, chose set 2 in their work. The data used by the Prosecutors' Bureau of the High Court (source 3) also show considerable discrepancy from those of the Police Bureau.

TABLE 14

THE NUMBER OF KOREANS ARRESTED AND PROSECUTED FOR VIOLATION OF THE PUBLIC SECURITY MAINTENANCE LAW, 1926–1935

	Arrested			*Prosecuted*		
Year	Cases	Persons	Average/ Case	Cases	Persons	Average/ Case
1926	45	356	7.9	27	157	5.8
1927	48	279	5.8	32	135	4.2
1928	168	1,415	8.4	98	494	5.0
1929	206	1,271	6.2	106	443	4.1
1930	252	2,661	10.6	140	690	4.9
1931	180	1,708	9.5	99	651	6.6
1932	254	4,381	17.2	159	1,011	6.4
1933	205	2,007	9.8	115	539	4.7
1934	145	2,065	14.2	84	518	6.2
1935	135	1,478	10.9	76	437	5.8
Total	1,638	17,621	10.7	936	5,075	5.4

SOURCE: Chōsen Sōtokufu, Kōtō Hōin, Kenjikyoku, Shisōbu (Thought Section Prosecutor's Bureau, High Court, Government General of Korea), *Shisō ihō* (Thought Report Series), no. 8 (September 1936), pp. 58–60.

NOTE: During the same period, only 89 Japanese were arrested for 21 cases.

Chapter 4

The Anti-Japanese Struggles and the Korean Communists in China

As we have seen, the earnest efforts of the Korean communists to organize an ongoing movement within Korea produced very unsatisfactory results. Even though socio-economic conditions were highly favorable for the communists, the Japanese police were too effective for the communist organizers. Even the most dedicated and scrupulous leader could not prevent the police from detecting the presence of his organization when his forces reached into the hundreds. Under such conditions, it was simply impossible for the Korean communists to implement the Comintern's exhortations.

The major shift in the Comintern line in 1935, calling for anti-Fascist united fronts in various countries, produced no visible change in Korea. A movement in the port city of Wonsan, South Hamgyŏng Province, headed by a few university faculty members and a veteran labor organizer (Ch'oe Yong-dal of Posŏng College, Yi Kang-guk and Chŏng Chin-t'ae of Keijo University, and Yi Chu-ha from the red labor union movement) did show some promise for the popular anti-Fascist front movement in Korea between 1936 and 1938, but it ended in late 1938 with the arrest of some 110 persons.[1] Korea in the meantime was rapidly turned into a logistic base for the Japanese military adventure into China and the Pacific. The Japanese systematically took measures to suppress all manifestations of Korean national consciousness, including the use of the Korean language, and began to force Korea and the Korean people to become an integral part of the Japanese war machinery. All the available human and natural resources were mobilized for the war effort. Increasingly stringent control was placed on the press, schools, churches, and all other organizations. The government took full control of the economy, and the movement of goods and the people was severely restricted.

After 1937, therefore, one could find the manifestation of Korean resistance against Japan only among the Koreans abroad, that is to say, the Koreans residing outside of Korea and Japan. The Koreans in Japan faced the identical situation as the Koreans in Korea and they were equally powerless.

At the end of 1932, the Japanese government estimated the Korean population abroad to be as follows: 400,000 in the Chientao region of Manchuria; 250,000 in other parts of Manchuria; 200,000 in Siberia; 3,500 in China proper; 5,000 in the Hawaiian islands; 10,000 in the United States; and 2,000 in Mexico.[2] But, except for some of the Koreans in Manchuria, particularly in the Chientao region, and in China proper, these Korean communities presented no serious concern for the Japanese government. Japan concluded a treaty with the Soviet Union in 1925, in which the Russians agreed not to permit any Koreans in their territory to engage in anti-Japanese activities. The Russians not only kept their word but in 1937 they uprooted all the Koreans in the Maritime provinces and shipped them to Uzbekistan and Kazakhstan, thus eliminating the need for the Japanese to be concerned about the possible use of Koreans against Japan.[3] The Koreans in North America, on the other hand, posed little threat to the Japanese empire. While nationalist sentiment against Japan was very strong and there were various organizations propagating anti-Japanese causes, Japan maintained friendly enough relations with the United States so that the Koreans there would not jeopardize Japan in any way.

The two areas that required constant vigilance of the Japanese police were China proper and the Chientao region of Manchuria. While the numbers of Koreans in such cities as Peking, Shanghai, and Nanking were not very large, they included some of the most determined anti-Japanese fighters. Since 1919, when the Korean Provisional Government had been organized in Shanghai, these Koreans persisted in sending agents to Japan and Korea to engage in terrorist and organizational activities. Among these Koreans were anarchists and communists, as well as those who simply sought Korean independence and were willing to follow any attractive alternative that presented itself. Some of them had established close connections with the Kuomintang; others had ties with the Chinese Communist Party.[4] Because of their fierce determination to oppose Japan and because of their geographic proximity to Korea and Japan, these Koreans were closely watched by the Japanese authorities.

The Japanese police also paid serious attention to the Koreans in Manchuria, for similar reasons. Ever since Japan had annexed Korea in 1910, the Chientao region in Manchuria had served as a political sanctuary for Korean nationalists and Communists, and in spite of the 1925 agreement with the Chang Tso-lin government whereby the latter agreed to suppress the "recalcitrant Koreans," and in spite of direct suppressive actions by the Japanese consular police and army units, the Korean nationalist and communist groups continued to operate there. Moreover, communist influence among the Koreans was substantial. In the early 1920s, the Koreans in this region had been affected by the propaganda and organizational movement of the Shanghai group under Yi Tong-hwi, as noted in Chapter One. In 1926, the Korean Communist Party in Seoul established its Manchurian General Bureau and expanded its organizational movement. The Japanese consular police arrested some 200 Korean communists in Chientao in 1927, but not all the communists were netted. In the summer and fall of 1930, Korean communists under the direction of the Chinese Communist Party carried out a mass riot in Lungching village and the neighboring towns and villages in Chientao, causing extensive damage to Japanese-owned government offices, power facilities, transportation and communication lines, and private homes.[5] Because of the large size of the Korean population in this region, and because of its geographic proximity to Korea, the Japanese had ample reasons to be concerned.

Communist activities among the Koreans in these two areas deserve to be studied in some detail, not only because they constituted important parts of the Korean communist movement but also because of the later significance of some of the leaders. The Yenan group of the post-1945 era emerged from the movement in China proper; and Kim Il-sŏng, the object of the cult of personality in North Korea since the late 1950s, emerged from the movement in Manchuria. Since both movements have been scrutinized in some detail elsewhere,[6] we shall discuss only the most salient aspects of them.

One feature that distinguished these groups from the other movements discussed so far is that they were parts of armed contingents fighting against Japan. Another feature is that they operated in Chinese territory as a part of the Chinese forces. These groups, however, operated in vastly different circumstances thousands of miles apart; there was no coordination, cooperation, or even contact between them. They were the products of their surroundings rather than the results of conscious planning in Moscow, Yenan, or Seoul.

The Korean communists had established ties with their Chinese counterparts as early as 1921, when Yi Tong-hwi's Shanghai group had allocated some of its Moscow funds to the Chinese communists. Later, when Voitinsky arrived in Shanghai and established the CCP, he had frequent contacts with the Korean communists, even though he devoted his major efforts to the Chinese movement. Therefore, some of the Korean leaders, such as Yŏ Un-hyŏng, developed close ties with Chinese communists. The Whampoa Military Academy also became a place of contact between young Koreans and Chinese communists; Korean cadets at the Academy had as instructors such prominent communists as Chou En-lai, Yeh Chien-ying, Nieh Jung-chen, and Ch'en Yi. These ties drew some of the Koreans into the CCP ranks, and when the CCP staged the Canton uprising in December 1927, some 150 to 200 Koreans played active roles.[7] We do not know how many Koreans joined in the Long March, but at least one, Mu Chŏng, survived the ordeal and attained a prominent position within the Chinese communist forces.[8]

While there may not have been many Koreans in Yenan after the Long March, the CCP and Mu Chŏng began to attract more of them after the outbreak of the second Sino-Japanese War in 1937. We do not know the exact circumstances of the beginning of the Korean unit, but the CCP permitted Mu to gather some 300 young Koreans and establish a Korean military unit which began to engage in battles in 1939. As the news of Mu's activities spread, more Koreans congregated around him. Some of the newcomers were from Hankow, where the Korean Volunteer Corps (Chosŏn Ŭiyong-dae) had been organized in October 1938 under the auspices of the Kuomintang government.

When the Korean contingent had grown to several hundred strong, in January 1941, they were organized into the North China Korean Youth Federation, with Mu Chŏng as its president. The immediate goal of the federation was to absorb Koreans arriving in North China. An initial declaration strongly urged both men and women to join the federation. It appealed to patriotism for Korea and stressed the possibilities for the liberation of Korea presented by the Sino-Japanese conflict. All revolutionary individuals and groups, regardless of ideology or religion, were to be welcomed.[9] At no point did the Korean groups in Yenan use overtly communist titles or sophistry, although the organizational and ideological life of the Koreans was closely patterned after that of their Chinese hosts. Thus, when the rectification campaign was launched in Yenan by the CCP in 1942, it was duplicated by the Koreans. In August 1942, the Youth Federation was renamed the Korean Independence League (Chosŏn Tongnip Tongmaeng) and the military unit was redesignated as the Korean Volunteer Army. Kim Tu-bong, a noted Korean scholar, went to Yenan from Chungking around this time and became chairman of the league's executive committee. Mu was appointed commander of the Volunteer Army. In November 1942, the North China Korean Youth Revolutionary School was opened in T'aihang, with Mu Chŏng serving as head of the school. It was renamed the North China Korean Revolutionary Military-Political School in late 1943. A report in the CCP organ in Yenan, *Chieh-fang Jih-pao* (Liberation Daily), in February 1944, indicated that "many Korean youth" from enemy-occupied areas had come to the school.[10] The Chinese communists regarded Mu Chŏng as the key figure among Korean revolutionaries. He was the only Korean to be given prominence in the Chinese communist press of this period, and his title of "Revolutionary Leader" made it apparent that the Chinese communist leaders of Yenan acknowledged him as the chief leader of the Korean independence movement. The young men in the Korean Independence League and the Volunteer Army fought and died in engagements with the Japanese army, but more of them apparently engaged in propaganda work against the Japanese army or interrogated Japanese prisoners for the CCP forces.[11]

Even though the number of individuals involved was small and their accomplishments were not very impressive when measured against the scale of the war being fought in China, this group was held in awe by many Koreans within Korea. Although the news within Korea was severely censored, some of the political and intellectual leaders were aware of the presence and activities of the Yenan group, and indeed a few of them went to join the revolutionaries. It should be noted that the Yenan group and another military group in Chungking under the Provisional Government known as the Restoration Army (Kwangbokkun) were the only remaining armed fighters against Japan that the Koreans had in 1945.

It is also important to note that most of the young men who joined the ranks of the Independence League and the Volunteer Army had received some college education. Most of the late arrivals in Yenan would have been deserters from the Japanese army, which had recruited a large number of Koreans since 1938, first as volunteers and then, beginning in August 1943, as conscripts. The initial group of young men being forced to "volunteer" were college students, many of whom deserted their Japanese units in China to join the anti-Japanese fighters either in Yenan or in Chungking. Therefore, they could quickly assume the role of officers in a larger army, as they indeed did in Manchuria and North Korea after the Japanese surrender. The Korean Volunteer Army, with a multitude of new recruits from North China and Manchuria, constituted an important element of the CCP's struggle against the Kuomintang after 1945. Many of these men—either with or without participating in the post-1945 civil war in China—served as officers of the North Korean army. The future of the top-echelon leaders of the Independence League will be described in the succeeding chapters.

The armed struggle of the Korean communists in Manchuria was conducted in vastly different circumstances. In contrast to the Yenan group, which was essentially a group in exile playing a subsidiary role for the Chinese hosts, the Korean communists in Manchuria constituted the mainstay of the communist movement there, although they were operating in a foreign country and under the direction of the CCP. The population in Chientao was predominantly Korean (as shown in Table 10, Chapter Three), and the Korean communists had dominated the communist movement there. Indeed, the Manchurian Province Committee of the CCP had not made much progress even after the Japanese takeover of Manchuria in 1931. Only since late 1932, through the anti-Japanese guerrilla movement, was the Manchurian Province Committee able to build a large following.

While the Korean activities constituted only a part of the movement, and they were largely confined in the southern part of Manchuria near the Korean-Manchurian border, it will be useful here to present an outline of the Chinese resistance movement in Manchuria after September 1931. This should enable us to place the Korean activities in proper perspective.[12]

As is well known, the Japanese army, which had been stationed along the South Manchuria Railway extending from Port Arthur in the south to Harbin in the north since the end of the Russo-Japanese war of

1904–1905, launched its major campaign to take over all of Manchuria in September 1931. It was soon able to occupy most of the major cities in Manchuria without encountering much resistance from the army of the Manchurian warlord Chang Hsueh-liang, but it soon faced strong spontaneous resistance movements organized by commanders of local military and police units, leaders of secret societies, and even bandit chieftains in various parts of Manchuria. Some of the anti-Japanese groups had as many as 50,000 men, but others were much smaller in size. Between 1932 and 1933, when the resistance movement was at its zenith, the anti-Japanese forces were estimated to be 360,000. These men, armed in varying degrees of sophistication, engaged the better armed and better trained Japanese army. Initially, the engagements involved large numbers of men on both sides, but gradually the anti-Japanese groups split into smaller groups. The Chinese fighters suffered severe casualties,[13] and by 1934, the total number of remaining fighters had dwindled to 40,000.[14]

It was in this atmosphere of fierce struggle that the CCP ordered its local units to organize armed guerrillas beginning in the spring of 1932. Initially, the party's radical policies against landlords, rich farmers, and the capitalist class, as well as its efforts to split the anti-Japanese groups to win over the lower-level troops, hampered the efforts of the communist guerrillas, but the Comintern's instruction of January 1933 to form a broad alliance with all anti-Japanese elements considerably eased the task of expanding their forces.[15] The military operations of the guerrillas were also significantly aided by the organization of anti-Japanese societies whose members supplied food, clothing, and other supplies as well as vital intelligence information. Soon the communist guerrillas began to surpass the non-communist groups in terms of military effectiveness and political following, and by 1936, most of the anti-Japanese movement in Manchuria was placed under the leadership of the CCP. While most of the non-communist groups operated alone, without much coordination among themselves and without the backing of popular organizations, the communist guerrillas were backed by the party organization and such mass organizations as anti-Japanese societies and farmers' associations. The communist guerrillas were also well indoctrinated and disciplined, which enabled them to fight more effectively and win the support of the masses, while the non-communist guerrillas lacked these qualities.

The communist guerrillas operated in areas between the South

Manchurian Railway and the Korean border on the one hand and the Chinese Eastern Railway and the Russian border on the other. These areas were ideal for the guerrillas because of the Changpai mountain range near the Korean border, the Wanta mountain range in the southeast, and the Lesser Hsingan mountain range in the northeast. The forests and swamps along the Sungari and Ussuri rivers also provided ideal sanctuaries for them. The "armies" created by the communists and other guerrillas were as follows:

The First People's Revolutionary Army. First Division established in August 1933 in P'anshih under Yang Ching-yü; moved to Tungpientao near the Korean border in the fall. Second Division established in November 1934 in P'anshih by the first regiment of the first division.

The Second People's Revolutionary Army. First Division established in February 1934, in Yenchi, in the Holung area of Chientao, under Wang Te-t'ai. Second Division established in May 1935, in the Hunch' un-Wangch'ing area of Chientao.

The Third People's Revolutionary Army. Established in January 1935, in Chuho, east of Harbin, by Chao Shang-chih.

The Fourth People's Revolutionary Army. First Division established in February 1935, in Mishan, near the Ussuri River by Li Yen-lu, a non-communist leader, with some communists. Second Division established in April and May of 1936, under Cheng Lu-yen, in Mishan or Jaoho near the Ussuri River.

The Fifth Anti-Japanese Allied Army. Established in February 1935 in Ningan, south of Mutanchiang, by Chao Pao-chung.

The Sixth Anti-Japanese Allied Army. Established in early 1936 in T'angyuan, west of Chiamussu on the Sungari River, under Hsia Yun-chieh.

The Seventh Anti-Japanese Allied Army. Established in 1936 in the Hulin-Jaoho area near the Ussuri River; headed by Li Pao-man, and later Ch'oe Sŏk-ch'ŏn (Ch'oe Yong-gŏn).

The Eighth Anti-Japanese Allied Army. Established in 1936 in Ilan south of T'angyuan (see the Sixth Army), under Hsieh Wen-tung, by anti-Japanese farmers. Hsieh surrendered in 1938.

The Ninth Anti-Japanese Allied Army. Established in 1936 in the Ilan-Poli area by Li Hua-t'ang, with the remnants of the old Chilin (warlord) army. Li surrendered in 1938.

The Tenth Anti-Japanese Allied Army. Established in Shulan, east of Chilin, by a small band of the Shan-lin-tui (Mountain Grove Unit) under Wang Ya-ch'en around 1938, but was soon destroyed by the Japanese forces.

The Eleventh Anti-Japanese Allied Army. Established in Ilan-T'angyuan area by Ch'i Ming-san with Shan-lin-tui members.[16]

After 1937 these armies went through an extensive reorganization. Evidently the communists felt the need to consolidate the scattered forces to achieve better coordination. The problem of attrition in the ranks would have loomed large also, as the Japanese launched intensive campaigns against them. Some of the armies existed in name only, and needed to be regrouped and reassigned. Therefore all the anti-Japanese forces in Manchuria were reorganized into three Route Armies. The first and second armies were grouped together in 1937 under the First Route Army with Yang Ching-yü as its commander; it was to continue its operation in the southeastern part of the Liaoning province. In 1938, the fourth, fifth, seventh, and eighth armies were grouped under the Second Route Army with Chou Pao-chung as commander; it was to continue its operation in the eastern part of the Chilin province. The third, sixth, ninth, and eleventh armies were consolidated into the Third Route Army in early 1939, with Li Ch'ao-lin (alias Chang Shou-ch'ien) as its commander; it was to continue its operations in the Heilunchiang province.[17]

There is no question that these men fought heroically. While the seventh to the eleventh armies appear to have been much smaller in size, all the other armies consisted of between 1,000 to 1,500 men at their peak strength, and most of them were surrounded by strong networks of mass organizations such as the various anti-Japanese societies and farmers' associations. Sometimes they fought frontal battles against the enemy using large numbers of men, but mostly they engaged in guerrilla warfare, attacking cities and towns held by the puppet regime of Manchukuo, destroying trains, trucks, and railroads, raiding mines, killing and kidnapping Japanese officials and residents, and otherwise harassing the Japanese and pro-Japanese Manchukuo forces. The extent of the Japanese concern can be seen by the large-scale anti-guerrilla campaigns of the winter of 1936, aimed against the communist (2,600 men) and non-communist forces (2,900 men) in Tungpientao on the western slope of the Ch'angpai mountain range; when the Japanese sent in 16,000 Manchukuo troops against them.[18] Principal casualties of this campaign on the anti-Japanese side were Wang Te-t'ai, the commander of the second army; Chou Shou-tung, who had succeeded Wang; Ch'ao Kuo-an, the second division commander of the first army; and Wang Feng-ke, the head of the Anti-Japanese Volunteers Army in Tungpientao, who used to be called the king of Tungpientao. In the winter of 1937, the Japanese dispatched some 25,000 troops, including a division of the Japanese army, to northern Manchuria where the third to the tenth anti-Japanese armies (total estimated strength, 12,000 to 13,000) were in operation.[19] Chao Shang-chih, the head of the third army, and Hsia Yun-chieh, the head of the sixth army, were among the casualties. The heads of the eighth army (Hsieh Wen-tung), ninth army (Li Hua-t'ang), and the fourth army (Cheng Lu-yen) surrendered. These, incidentally, were non-communist leaders. In 1939, the Japanese again launched a massive military and political campaign against the guerrillas remaining in the Ch'angpai mountain range (Chilin, Chientao, and T'unghua provinces under the Manchukuo's administrative system), pouring in Japanese and Manchukuo troops and the police forces. The plan adopted by the Kwantung Army headquarters, with the direct participation of its chief of staff, involved 30 million yen (about 15 million dollars) and the campaign lasted two and a half years.[20] Food and intelligence sources were cut off from the guerrillas by collecting all the villagers in remote areas into so-called "collective villages," and the guerrillas were pursued continuously during the winter months, so that they had no chance to recuperate or search for food. The guerrillas were pursued not only on the ground but also from the air. Both Yang Ching-yü, the most renowned hero of the anti-Japanese movement in Manchuria and the commander of the First Route Army, and his deputy, Wei Cheng-min, were killed in action. Yang was killed on February 23, 1940, leaving many a legend.[21]

The intensity of the struggles can also be seen from the statistics provided in Table 15. The increase in the number of anti-Japanese fighters reported by the Japanese in 1935 is undoubtedly due to the intensified activities of the communist forces. The phenomenal growth of the number of anti-Japanese fighters reported in 1937 undoubtedly reflected the intensified anti-Japanese feeling among the Chinese population after the Japanese launched the second Sino-Japanese war in July that year.

TABLE 15

THE ANTI–JAPANESE STRUGGLE IN MANCHURIA AND LOSSES SUFFERED BY THE ANTI–JAPANESE FORCES, 1932–1940

Year	Number of Appearances of "Insurgents"	Cumulative Number of "Insurgents" Reported	"Insurgents" per Appearance	Killed	Wounded	Captured	Rifles Captured	Ammunition Captured (Rounds)	Horses Captured
1932	3,816	3,774,184	989.0	7,591	5,160	831	3,642	8,238	1,558
1933	13,072	2,668,633	204.1	8,728	2,381	1,461	5,970	174,288	2,731
1934	13,395	900,204	67.2	8,909	4,264	1,435	3,153	36,107	2,889
1935	39,150	1,783,855	45.5	13,338	11,815	2,703	6,265	91,780	7,248
1936	36,517	1,555,558	42.6	10,713	7,988	1,783	5,300	72,736	4,251
1937	25,487	10,355,577	406.3	7,663	5,242	1,298	2,871	69,081	3,465
1938	13,110	468,884	35.8	3,693	2,876	799	2,609	57,182	1,721
1939	6,547	186,071	28.4	3,168	1,753	496	2,870	51,158	1,287
1940	3,667	132,660	36.2	2,140	1,873	545	1,807	48,274	997
Total	154,761	21,825,626	141.0	65,943	43,352	11,351	34,487	608,844	26,127

SOURCE: Manshūkoku-shi Hensan Kankokai (Society to Compile and Publish the History of Manchukuo), *Manshūkoku-shi* (History of Manchukuo), Tokyo, 1971, p. 312.

NOTE: This table covers the activities of both communist and non-communist groups.

What role did the Koreans play in these bitter struggles against Japanese imperialism? How shall we assess the overall significance of their activities in general? To begin with, the role of the Koreans can be discussed in terms of (1) communist activities before the beginning of the organization of the guerrilla forces, (2) the communist role in the initiation of the guerrilla forces, (3) the men who constituted the rank and file of the "armies," and (4) the leadership provided.

There is no doubt that the communist organizations established by the Koreans before 1930 played a very important role in the initiation and continuation of communist guerrilla activities. Before the Korean communists were absorbed into the CCP in 1930, the Chinese communists had not been able to recruit very many members even in the major cities of Manchuria, and they made virtually no attempt to recruit members from the towns and villages in remote areas. But various Korean communist groups had penetrated into Korean communities in remote areas and established their branches. This was the case even outside of the Chientao region, where the Korean population constituted an overwhelming majority. Thus there were Korean communist organizations in P'anshih in southern Manchuria, where the first army established its headquarters; Chuho in the east of Harbin, where the third army was established; Mishan near the Ussuri River, where the fourth army had its beginnings; Ningan in the east of Chilin, where the fifth army originated; T'angyuan, the headquarters of the sixth army; and Jaoho, the birthplace of the seventh army. The presence of these communists gave rise to anti-Japanese societies, which in turn led to the organization of anti-Japanese guerrillas who eventually expanded into larger forces. Even though the various armies were founded and headed by the Chinese, the origins of many of them can be traced back to Korean activities. Various mass organizations, such as anti-Japanese societies, peasant associations, and communist youth leagues were also led by the Koreans, and provided important support to the guerrillas.

We have already indicated that many of the armies sprung from the anti-Japanese guerrillas organized by the Koreans. Perhaps the most important of these was the organization of the Northeast Volunteer Army by the P'anshih Prefectural Committee of the CCP in May 1932. At that time, there were forty Koreans and thirty Chinese in the "army," a reconstituted body of red militiamen and a guerrilla unit under the prefectural committee. This small unit was reorganized in October into the South Manchurian Guerrilla Unit of the Chinese Red Army, 32nd

Army, with 230 men, of which 80 were Koreans. (We do not know where the designation of the 32nd Army came from.) This unit was headed by a Korean by the name of Yi Hong-gwang, who received special mention from Chu Teh in Yenan in September 1942[22] and was commemorated by the citizens of Shenyang along with Yang Ching-yü at a mass rally in February 1946.[23] This unit was converted into the first army of the Northeast People's Revolutionary Army in August 1933, setting a pattern for other areas.[24]

These beginnings, and the fact that a large number of Koreans living in Manchuria held strong anti-Japanese feelings and had numerous grievances of a socio-economic nature, made it inevitable that Koreans would constitute an important element of the guerrilla forces. In 1935 the CCP leaders exercised harsh discrimination against the Koreans for unfounded but strongly held suspicions that Korean leaders and troops were in fact collaborating with the Japanese authorities.[25] Until that time, however, large numbers of Koreans could be found in various guerrilla groups and party branches, often in leadership roles. In the first army, for example, most of the Korean contingent held high positions in spite of the fact that they constituted only one-fourth of the total forces.[26] This, according to the Japanese, was because the Koreans have undergone long periods of revolutionary training, in both nationalist and communist activities. Of course, as the guerrilla movement expanded and greater numbers of the Chinese masses joined the ranks, the Korean influence waned. The conscious discrimination exercised by the Chinese leaders, of course, had a great impact.

Even after 1935, however, a large number of Koreans remained, as leaders as well as within the ranks. The Second Army, in particular, was predominantly Korean because of its area of origin (Chientao) and its field of operation. Thus Wei Cheng-min, the deputy commander of the First Route Army reporting to the Chinese representative of the Comintern in April 1940,[27] just before he was killed in action, mentioned Kim Il-sŏng as the commander of the Second Area Army of the three area armies in the First Route Army, Sŏ Ch'ŏl as the chief of the Medical Office, O Paek-yong as the commander of the 7th Regiment, Ch'oe Hyŏn as the commander of the 13th regiment, and An Kil as the political commissar of the 14th regiment. Of course, by this time, army unit designations were more euphemistic than ever. An area army probably did not contain more than two or three hundred troops. Feng Chung-yün, the Chinese author and the veteran leader of the Third Route

Army, referred to Kim Il-sŏng as the remaining leader of the First Route Army after the death of Yang Ching-yü, and Ch'oe Sŏk-ch'ŏn (Ch'oe Yong-gŏn) as the commander of the Seventh Army. Other Korean leaders mentioned by Feng include Ch'oe Hyŏn, An Kil, Sŏ Ch'ŏl, and Pak Tŏk-san (Kim Il) in the First Route Army; Kang Shin-t'ae (Kang Kŏn ?) and Kim Kwang-hyŏp in the Second Route Army; and Kim Ch'aek in the Third Route Army. Two other Korean communists, Pak Ki-song and Hŏ Hyŏng-sik, were also mentioned by Feng in connection with the Third Route Army, but they were killed in action before 1945.[28]

Thus the Korean contribution in the leadership of the guerrilla armies in all theatres of operation was substantial. It should be noted here that all the surviving Korean veterans returned to Korea after 1945, and occupied leading positions in the north Korean party, government, and the army. It should be added that the situation in Manchuria after 1940 became quite impossible even for the most seasoned communist guerrillas to survive. Even though both the Chinese and Korean communist sources do not mention their retreat to Siberia, a Japanese source noted the confirmation of Kim Il-sŏng's retreat to the Russian territory with six followers in February 1941.[29] This information is most likely to be accurate.[30] It is also quite likely that many other Chinese and Korean veterans of this period retreated to Siberia for rest and recuperation, although it is also possible that some others stayed to continue small-scale and sporadic activities.[31]

The assessment of the significance of these guerrilla fighters is likely to be colored by one's ideological outlook and historical perspective on the entire history of the Korean nationalist and communist movements. The dedication, determination, courage, perseverance, and skill of these guerrilla fighters, of course, deserve high praise. While the full details of their activities were not reported in Korea at the time, the exploits of Kim Il-sŏng and Ch'oe Hyŏn on the Sino-Korean border—particularly Kim's raid of the border town of Pojŏn in June 1937 and Ch'oe's raid of Musan in the same year—were widely reported in the censored press, and they considerably encouraged nationalistic feeling among Koreans everywhere. Since it was already nearly thirty years after the Japanese had taken Korea, and since the Japanese authorities had all but suffocated any expression of nationalist sentiment in Korea by then, the news of the raid and the subsequent revelation that there were supporting organizations in the border area of Kapsan and Samsu is likely to have made a significant impact. A legend of Kim Il-sŏng spread among a considerable part of the population. Kim was frequently portrayed as an aged hero of the generation of Kim Ku and Syngman Rhee (both sexagenarians) or older, perhaps a survivor of the anti-Japanese struggle before and after the Japanese annexation in Korea in 1910. There appears to have been a legendary fighter by the same name around that time in the border area, and Kim's sudden appearance in 1937 compounded the confusion. (Kim Il-sŏng, incidentally, was born Kim Sŏng-ju and took the new name in the early 1930s.) In any event, it is unquestionable that Kim Il-sŏng's exploits had a tonic effect on Korean nationalism in the late 1930s. Through Kim's activities, and others like them, many Koreans could vicariously defy Japanese oppression.

Beyond this, however, the activities of the Manchurian guerrillas left no tangible results. By 1941, their activities were over. They left no concrete political or military organization, either in Manchuria or Korea. Thousands of Koreans had become martyrs or prisoners trying to build a communist party and a communist army—or simply trying to defy the Japanese aggressors—but the Japanese empire remained as undisturbed as before. Kim Il-sŏng was in exile in Siberia, as were many other Korean nationalists and communists in Chungking, Yenan, and various cities in Hawaii and the continental United States. In fact, those in other places were more numerous and were more actively engaged in anti-Japanese activities after 1941 than Kim Il-sŏng.

To argue that Kim Il-sŏng was the only true leader of the Korean revolution, or that Korean communism was the product solely of Kim's wisdom and efforts, as the Korean communists have been doing since the 1960s, is simply to ignore the facts. But there can be no doubt about Kim's acumen, ability, and luck—as can be seen from the events that followed the Japanese surrender on August 15, 1945.

Chapter 5

The Beginning of the New Era in North Korea

Stalin told Milovan Djilas in April 1945, "This war is not as in the past; whoever occupies a territory also imposes on it his own social system. Everyone imposes his own system as far as his army can reach. It cannot be otherwise."[1] And so when Soviet forces occupied North Korea in August 1945, they imposed their own political system. It could not be otherwise. North Korea was destined to have a political system very closely patterned after that of the Soviet Union. The Communist Party would hold all key posts in the government and allow very little power to the opposition groups.

But who should be placed at the top of the party and government and how power should be distributed among the top contenders were important questions that the Korean communists had never been able to discuss in collectivity until 1945. Indeed, until a few months after the Japanese surrender in August 1945, the Korean communists could not even know for certain who would be the top contenders for power. They also could not know what role other fraternal parties, such as those of the Soviet Union and China, might play in the selection of the leadership and policy lines. And no one would have predicted that the thirty-eighth parallel proposed by the United States government as a temporary line of division between the two occupying powers would turn into a permanent line of division and affect the course of politics among Korean communists. Even the Soviet leaders themselves could not have predicted in August 1945 how the United States and the Soviet Union might resolve potential areas of conflict when the two armies ended their alleged mission of disarming the Japanese forces in Korea. It was only in December of that year that the Moscow conference of the three foreign ministers (including that of Great Britain) agreed on a formula for the future of Korea. The Soviet commander of the occupying forces in Pyongyang may have had a few contingency plans about Korea within the broad framework of Stalin's comment to Djilas, but even he could not have predicted the future course of events.

It became very clear soon after the Soviet Army marched into North Korea, however, that the Soviet command would have the strongest voice in the choice of the Korean communist leadership, and that its choice was Kim Il-sŏng. He was fortunate in that he had been forced to flee to Soviet territory in 1941. The Soviet leaders would have had ample time to listen to his reports and reminiscences and evaluate him. We do not know whether Ch'oe Yong-gŏn (Ch'oe Sŏk-ch'ŏn), Kim Ch'aek, and others also spent their final years of the war in the Soviet Union, but there is no doubt that the Soviet leaders favored Kim Il-sŏng over all others as the top leader. This can be seen from the mass rally held in Pyongyang in his honor on October 14, 1945.

But would the Soviet command have insisted on Kim Il-sŏng even if Korea had not been divided and if the Korean communists could operate freely throughout Korea? One cannot be very sure of this. Those communists recently released from prison or emerging from the underground began to reconstruct the party in Seoul soon after the Japanese surrender, and on September 11, they publicly announced the creation of a Korean Communist Party (KCP). The clear choice of these communists for their leader was Pak Hŏn-yŏng, the veteran of the Irkutsk group in Shanghai, of the Japanese prison in 1921, and of the first KCP organized in Korea in 1925. Kim Il-sŏng paid homage to the primacy of Pak in clear language on October 13, when the first meeting of the North Korean communist representatives, known as the Five Provinces Conference, was held in Pyongyang.[2] It is, of course, possible to see this gesture as a maneuver by Kim and the Soviet command to stall for time. In the end, Kim Il-sŏng could have emerged as a victor even if Korea had not been divided. But, had Pak Hŏn-yŏng and his men been allowed to engage in the internal competition on equal terms, Kim might not have emerged as the victor so soon. Since Pak's loyalty to Stalin was unquestionable, the Soviet command would not have found it necessary to dispose of him in favor of Kim Il-sŏng.

All this, of course, is conjecture. The Soviet command evidently decided that the communist organization in North Korea should be consolidated under a single command without waiting for the outcome of negotiations with the United States on Korea's future. On October 13, at the Five Provinces Conference of the Korean communists, the North Korean Bureau was established. At the same time, a seventeen-member North Korean Committee of the KCP was established under a presidium.[3] Even though Kim Il-sŏng stressed the subordinate character of the North Korean Bureau to the Seoul headquarters, it was clear that the leaders in Seoul could no longer reach the members in North Korea without going through the new bureau. This in fact meant that Kim Il-sŏng attained autonomy in North Korea through the maneuver. The Soviet command also established the Five Provinces Administrative Bureau in October as a governing mechanism for its zone of occupation.

Meanwhile the communists in South Korea were having problems with the American occupation authorities in Seoul. The problems began on the day that American forces landed in Korea, September 8. Immediately after the Japanese surrender, and three weeks before the arrival of the American forces, the Preparation Committee for the Construction of the Nation, or Kŏnguk Chunbi Wiwŏnhoe, abbreviated as Kŏn-Chun, was created on August 15, in Seoul, by Yŏ Un-hyŏng. The Japanese were interested in maintaining order and protecting Japanese lives after the surrender, while the Koreans were interested in building a political organization. Kŏn-Chun's Vice Chairman, An Chae-hong, broadcast the news of the establishment of the Committee on August 16 over the nationwide network suggesting that the Koreans were in full control of the government and its policies. People's Committees (or Kŏn-Chun branches) and Public Security Units sprang up in various localities to take over governmental and police power from the Japanese, and for a while, the Kŏn-Chun was looked upon by many as the central government of the Koreans.[4] The leaders of the Kŏn-Chun, however, held a hastily convened All-Nation People's Congress on September 6, two days before the landing of the American forces, and established the Korean People's Republic. The American commander refused to recognize not only the republic, which stood on very fragile legal and political ground, but also the local committees which included most of the leading elites in each locality. This was the beginning of the friction between the KCP and the U.S. occupation authorities which did much damage to both sides. The KCP was involved because the People's Republic was generally regarded as a creature of the KCP.

The Soviet command in Pyongyang voiced no opinion on the republic in spite of the position of the KCP in Seoul. Perhaps the fact that Kim Il-sŏng was not assigned a cabinet post in the republic's "cabinet" and the fact that the People's Congress had been hastily convened without proper procedure may explain the silence on the part of the Soviet command. As it became clear in 1947 and 1948, the Soviet command clearly favored a more deliberate and orderly process for creating a state.

In the meantime, preparations were underway to create a governmental mechanism for all of North Korea. Unlike the American occupation in the south, which decided to use its own military personnel in direct administration of South Korea, the Soviet command decided to govern its territory through the people's committees. In theory, the Korean people were on their own, but in practice, Soviet presence was felt everywhere. This was, of course, to be expected; it was the Soviet commander who held complete authority over North Korea. He was not likely to allow the political situation in his territory to go counter to the Soviet policy. It was his decision that the people's committees should govern their territories but they should be under Soviet supervision. The people's committees would be allowed maximum latitude if their composition and policies were in line with Soviet policy. Otherwise, the Soviet command would exercise its power to correct the situation. Thus the Pyongyang branch of the Kŏn-Chun, for example, had contained only two communists out of more than twenty members, reflecting the weakness of the communists in this area, but the Soviet command instructed it to change its name to the People's Political Committee and reorganize it with sixteen communists and sixteen non-communists. The Chinnamp'o branch of Kŏn-Chun, located in the estuary of Taedong River, was also reorganized to consist of eight from the original Kŏn-Chun, eight from the Communist Party, and five from the local communist-controlled labor union. A similar situation developed in the Hwanghae province near the 38th parallel.[5] In North and South Hamgyŏng provinces, where the communists were more numerous and excercised stronger influence, such needs did not arise. The aim of the

Soviet command was to create a coalition of communists and non-communists, a united front to make it appear that the political mechanism in the Soviet territory received the full backing of the people. It was not necessary nor desirable for Soviet personnel to be present in these committees. The Communist Party members in these committees effectively served the interests of the North Korean Bureau of the KCP, which in turn was controlled by the Soviet command.

It should be noted in passing that this system was inherently more effective and met with less resistance from the populace than the system of government instituted by the United States occupation in South Korea. Although American military personnel were directly assigned to various governmental institutions in South Korea, they had no knowledge of Korea or the Korean language, and were easily maneuvered by interpreters and self-seeking individuals. An irony here is that the U.S. authorities ruled Japan in much the same way as the Soviet authorities ruled North Korea, with much better results.

Having laid the foundation at the local level, an Enlarged Conference of the representatives of the North Korean Democratic Parties, Social Organizations, the Five Provinces Bureau, and the People's Political Committees was convened in Pyongyang on February 8, 1946, to create a region-wide political structure. Kim Il-sŏng presented the keynote speech, in which he declared the need for a planned unified development of North Korean politics, economy, and culture, and called for the creation of a North Korean Provisional People's Committee. This committee was to serve in North Korea until Korean unification had been accomplished. Thus, the North Korean government came into being. The committee in quick succession enacted the Land Reform Act in March 1946, the Labor Ordinance in June, a law equalizing the rights of men and women in August, and in the same month, another law nationalizing industries, railroads, other transport facilities, and banks. Small-scale private enterprises, however, were to be encouraged. In October, the committee announced its "Decision Concerning the Protection of Private Ownership in Industrial and Commercial Activity and Procedures for Encouraging the Development of Private Initiative."[6] Regardless of the outcome of the Soviet-American negotiations, upon which depended the unification of Korea, North Korea was to complete the "bourgeois democratic" revolution in preparation for its transition to the socialist stage. Kim Il-sŏng had declared at the KCP Northern Bureau's third Enlarged Executive Committee meeting on December 17,

1945, that the Korean communists, by uniting with "all democratic parties and social organizations," would build a "strong democratic base" in North Korea.[7] Incidentally, Kim was elected the first secretary of the North Korean Bureau at this executive committee meeting, according to a communist source.[8] Kim was also elected chairman of the Provisional People's Committee. Hyŏn Chun-Hyŏk, a native communist (as opposed to a returned exile), was very popular among the radical intellectuals and militant nationalists, and hence could have been Kim's rival for the KCP's secretary position, but he was assassinated on September 28, two weeks after trenchant criticism was directed against the conduct of the South P'yŏngan District of the KCP, of which Hyŏn was the head.[9] Cho Man-sik, the Christian elder and sometime president of *Chosŏn Ilbo* (Korean Daily), was the most popular leader in North Korea, and hence had served as head of the Pyongyang branch of the Kŏn-Chun as well as head of the Five Provinces Administration Bureau since October 1945; but he was eliminated from the scene in January 1946 because of his adamant opposition to the Moscow agreement of the three foreign ministers in December, by which it was agreed to impose a trusteeship upon Korea.[10] It is quite possible that the Soviet command wished to keep Cho Man-sik on the scene by appointing him chairman of the Provisional People's Committee as well as head of the Democratic Party that had been organized. It would have been useful for the Soviet command to have him head the united front government rather than assigning all the leadership positions to Kim Il-sŏng, or to have Ch'oe Yong-gŏn (known as Ch'oe Sŏk-ch'ŏn during his Manchurian guerrilla days) as the head of the Democratic Party. But Cho was uncooperative, and unlike the United States, the Soviet Union was not willing to change its stand on the issue of imposing trusteeship over Korea. With Cho Man-sik taken away for confinement, or whatever other forms of punishment the Soviet command decided to impose upon him, most of the non-communist leaders decided to flee to South Korea. After early 1946, North Korea became a dangerous place for non-communist activists to engage in political activities. Soviet-American relations were rapidly deteriorating, and this was directly reflected on both halves of Korea.

The movement to create a united front, or a semblance of it, continued, however. The North Korean Democratic National United Front was established in June 1946 as a mechanism to unite the entire North Korean people and to construct a new and democratic Korea. All "democratic" organizations in North Korea were brought under the front, which was to serve as a "common consultative organization." The front, however, was to make very little impact, either as a communist tool or a tool of its member organizations. All the social organizations brought together as members of the front were too obviously subservient to the Communist Party for anyone to pay much attention to it.

In August 1946, the North Korean Bureau of the Communist Party made another important move which not only strengthened the position of the communists in North Korea but substantially changed their relationship with the KCP leadership in Seoul. It was the amalgamation of the KCP's North Korean Bureau with the returnees from Yenan, who had established the New People's Party (Shinmin-dang) and operated separately from the KCP. While the membership of this party was relatively small, it had included more of the locally influential persons who could be identified as opinion-makers in their communities.[11] While the KCP attracted those who had played some roles in the various communist movements under the Japanese, and hence was very strongly rooted in the Hamgyŏng and Kangwon provinces in the eastern half of North Korea, it had a weaker base in the P'yŏngan and Hwanghae provinces in the western half. While the ideological purity or revolutionary zeal of the New People's Party members was suspect, they were better educated and wielded more influence among the people in areas where the KCP had no mass base.[12] In order to build an effective political mechanism in the Soviet-occupied territory, it was necessary to bring these elements under the same rubric with the KCP and subject them to the same command structure. The newly amalgamated party was named the North Korean Workers' Party (Puk-Chosŏn Nodong-dang).

The establishment of the North Korean Workers' Party (NKWP) can be seen as a step toward the consolidation of communist strength in North Korea, as well as an attempt to expand its influence across wider segments of the population. It must be noted also, however, that the action signified basic changes in the relationship between the communist leaders in the south, who had been acknowledged as the legitimate leaders of the entire Korean communist movement, and those in the north, who were supposedly under the direction of the southern (or central) leaders. It is significant that the leaders of the New People's Party, who allegedly proposed the amalgamation, did not submit the proposal to the Seoul headquarters but only to the North Korean Bureau of the KCP. The Korean communists also frequently used the title of North Korean Communist Party before the NKWP was created, although it is not certain whether the new title was introduced simply for the sake of convenience. In any event, by establishing the NKWP, the communists in the north officially detached themselves from the authority of the "central leaders" in Seoul, who had ceased to exercise control over the North Korean communists since the establishment of the North Korean Bureau. The communists in the south went through the process of amalgamation with the New People's Party there about this time, creating the South Korean Workers' Party (SKWP) in November. All this meant that the NKWP and the SKWP were now on an equal footing rather than the former being subordinate to the latter. Thus, the change in power relationship among the communists—particularly that between Kim Il-sŏng and Pak Hŏn-yŏng—was effected while the attention of the public was focused on the creation of the new parties. While Kim Il-sŏng yielded the position of chairman of the NKWP to Kim Tu-bong, the former head of the New People's Party, and occupied the post of vice-chairman, he still remained at the helm of the new political structure.

What were to be the goals of the new party? Kim Il-sŏng asserted at the inaugural conference of the NKWP that the basic task was to establish a unified, democratic, independent Korea as quickly as possible. That required the purging of all "pro-Japanese, fascist, and reactionary forces" and the application of "fundamental democratic reforms throughout the nation." For these purposes, North Korea would be "the base and the main force." This required the creation of a mass party, uniting workers, farmers, and the intelligentsia. The KCP had not been able to mobilize the intelligentsia in any comprehensive manner in the past, and the amalgamation of the New People's Party made this possible. He also attacked a new national enemy, "a new group of running dogs and national traitors nesting in South Korea who wanted to sell Korea out as a colony of monopoly capitalism." A resolute struggle against all these enemies was proclaimed.[13] The NKWP was to develop into a "combat unit of the working masses and their vanguard." He also equated the "liberation of South Korea" with complete independence for Korea. "Only if we completely liberate South Korea," said Kim Il-sŏng, "can there be any full independence for Korea."[14]

The institutional foundation laid and the direction of the party and government established, the Korean communists earnestly set about to consolidate their power. The NKWP launched an intensive campaign to swell its ranks, and by August 1947, a year after its inauguration, the membership nearly doubled to 680,000. By early 1949, it reached 800,000.[15] The party also moved ahead with the task of building its subsidiary organizations, such as the Labor Union (designated Puk-Chosŏn Chik-ŏp Tongmaeng, or the North Korean Occupational League), the Farmers' League, Democratic Youth League, and Democratic Women's League. These were to become the route through which the population would be mobilized and indoctrinated for the cause of the socialist revolution.

The efforts toward building the party and its supporting organizations were accompanied by governmental institution-building. The North Korean Provisional People's Committee issued a decree on September 5, 1946, calling for elections on November 3 of representatives to municipal, prefectural, and provincial People's Committees. All "democratic" parties, public organizations, and societies were given the right to nominate candidates, who were then screened by the United Front, which nominated a candidate for each office. The voters were given the right to vote either for or against the candidate. According to official accounts, 99.6 percent of the registered voters participated, and 97 percent of the candidates chosen by the United Front were elected. One-third of the 3,459 representatives thus elected then met in a General Assembly of People's Committees in February 1947 to establish a permanent People's Assembly with 237 members, which proceeded to create a permanent North Korean People's Committee. This committee, legitimatized through these "democratic" elections, emerged as the official governing body for North Korea.[16] When no progress was made in the Soviet-American negotiations, and preparations were made to create a separate state in South Korea, the North Korean General Assembly called for a nationwide election in August 1948 to elect delegates to the Supreme People's Assembly. The communists later alleged that 77.8 percent of the eligible electorate in South Korea participated in the underground election to elect 1,000 delegates who met in the north Korean city of Haeju to elect 360 representatives to the Supreme People's Assembly which had a total membership of 572. Thus, the Democratic People's Republic of Korea (DPRK), proclaimed by the Supreme People's Assembly in September, claimed to represent all the Korean people, in both north and south Korea. Kim Tu-bong, the Yenan leader, was elected chairman of the Presidium of the Supreme People's Assembly; Kim Il-sŏng was elected Premier, with vast powers over the executive branch of the government; Pak Hŏn-yŏng, the South Korean leader now in exile, was appointed a vice-premier and Foreign

Minister. It should be added in this connection that the workers' parties of north and south Korea were amalgamated into one party in June 1949, with headquarters in Pyongyang. In contrast to cases in previous periods, the list of the leaders of the new Korean Workers' Party (KWP) accurately reflected the power distribution among the top communist leaders. Thus Kim Il-sŏng, the former vice-chairman of the NKWP, was elected chairman of the KWP. Kim Tu-bong, the former chairman of the NKWP, and Pak Hŏn-yŏng, and Hŏ Ka-i, were elected vice-chairmen.

In the American zone of occupation, general elections were held in May 1948 to elect members of the National Assembly, which quickly established the Republic of Korea (ROK). This government also claimed authority over the entire peninsula, although this legislature had left one hundred seats vacant for North Korean representatives to be elected at an appropriate time. These actions left no doubt that two states had been created in Korea, and that the claims of each state conflicted with those of the other. Unlike the case in Germany, where the two governments claimed jurisdiction only over the territory upon which they exercised actual power, in Korea the constitutions declared that the government created across the 38th parallel was ipso facto illegitimate, falsely claiming authority over the territory which it controlled. Unless both sides were willing to revise their constitutions, the conflict could not be resolved without the destruction of one of the governments. Thus the institution-building process in both north and south Korea was intricately connected with the question of unification, which became an obsessive issue for the Korean people.

But how could South Korea be liberated from the "new group of running dogs and national traitors nesting in South Korea," as Kim Il-sŏng had called for in his speech of August 1946? This was obviously a question of the most serious concern for the North Korean leaders and their supporters. The KCP had been in existence in South Korea since August 1945, and its successor, the South Korean Workers' Party, had considerable support from the workers and peasants there, but the communists were not in a position to overthrow the ROK government headed by Syngman Rhee. While the incipient ROK army was ill-trained and ill-equipped, it was able to quell a military revolt launched by a communist-led regiment in October 1948. Because the South Korean government suppressed the communists with vengeance, the communists had little hope of gaining control of the government through electoral procedures. It was true that the ROK government was overburdened by socio-economic problems it had inherited from the U.S. military government and the Rhee government was rapidly losing the support of the electorate, as shown in the general elections held in April 1950, but the government that would replace Rhee was not expected to be any more sympathetic to communists.

It is possible, therefore, that the North Korean leaders and their allies decided that efforts toward liberating South Korea through military conquest should take place as soon as possible, before the South Korean leaders had a chance to build a workable system and strengthen their armed forces. Prolongation of the stalemate would also emasculate whatever underground supporters the communists had possessed in the south. While North Korea had built a streamlined political system since 1946 under the Soviet aegis and the indigenous leaders were in full control of their political and economic resources, Syngman Rhee had acquired power only in 1948, and the political system under him could not be expected to mobilize sufficient human and natural resources to counter a major offensive from the North. In March of 1950 the United States Congress authorized $10,970,000 to strengthen the South Korean Army, which could soon make it a more formidable opponent, but in the summer of 1950 the South Korean forces were not expected to match those of North Korea in terms of firepower. While the North Koreans possessed T-34 medium tanks, YAK fighters, and attack bombers, the South Koreans had no airforce nor even one tank. The ROK did not have a military treaty with the United States, and high officials of the United States had publicly declared in January 1950 that the United States would not defend South Korea.

Krushchev's assertion that the initiative for the war came from Kim Il-sŏng, and that he told Stalin that with one poke of a bayonet an internal explosion would be set off in South Korea and the people would be liberated from Syngman Rhee's rule, therefore, sounds credible.[17] It is true that the South Korean leaders, including the defense minister, had openly boasted of the ability of the South Korean army to smash the North Korean forces, and frequently advocated a march to the north. But there is no room to doubt that the South Korean forces were inferior to those of North Korea in every manner.

In the early morning of June 25, 1950, the Korean People's Army, the armed forces of the DPRK, launched a massive assault on South Korea. The North Koreans claim that the assault was in retaliation against provocations from South Korea, which attacked the North Korean forces first. According to official North Korean historians:

> At dawn on June 25, 1950, the U.S. imperialists, who had been preparing for a long time, ordered their henchmen Syngman Rhee clique to start an armed aggression on the Democratic People's Republic of Korea.[18] When the enemy crossed the 38th parallel, the government of the D.P.R.K. demanded the puppet Syngman Rhee clique to immediately stop the adventurous war gamble, warning them that should they fail to do so the Government of the D.P.R.K. would take a decisive measure to deal with them and subsequently the whole responsibility for the consequences would fall on them.[19]

If this were indeed the case, there is no record that such a warning was ever issued. Nor did Kim Il-sŏng refer to the warning in his broadcast of June 26, although he alleged on that occasion that the "puppet army of South Korea" had launched an "all-out offensive" and that the DPRK government had ordered the People's Army to start a "decisive counteroffensive action."[20] It is significant that Kim ended his broadcast by saying that "the time has come to reunify our country. Let us march forward valiantly with firm confidence in victory."[21] He referred to the war, which was to last until July 1953, as the "Just Fatherland Liberation War for Freedom and Independence."

Victory indeed seemed within reach of the communists in the early months of the war. Seoul, the South Korean capital, was taken on the fourth day of the war, June 28, and the North Korean forces swept down the peninsula without much difficulty. By early August, the battles were being fought in P'ohang at the 36th parallel north latitude and near Hyŏpch'ŏn at the 35th parallel. The Pusan perimeter, to which the South Korean and American forces were confined after August 4, consisted of a territory 90 miles long and 60 miles wide. (The first contingents of Americans landed in Korea on July 1.) The rest of the entire peninsula was in the hands of the communists. While Kim Il-sŏng was wrong to assume, as Khrushchev claimed he did, that with one poke of a bayonet an internal explosion would be set off in South Korea, his military plans had been excellent. The only unforeseen event in the war plan was the swift decision of the United States to commit her forces in support of South Korea. On June 26, President Truman had ordered the use of American planes and naval vessels against the North Korean forces, and on June 30, American ground troops were committed.

American leaders feared that inaction in Korea would be interpreted as appeasement of communist aggression elsewhere in the world.[22] They were determined that the Republic of Korea should not be vanquished. The North Korean forces were not able to break the Pusan perimeter, and as General MacArthur launched his amphibious movement with the Inchon landing on September 15, which severed the North Korean supply lines and isolated the North Korean forces south of the Han River, the entire war scene abruptly changed. Korea was not to be reunified by force.[23] The war was to last until July 27, 1953, when a cease fire agreement was signed at Panmunjŏm. By then, the war had involved the People's Republic of China, which had sent a massive force of "volunteers," the Soviet Union, which had dispatched air force divisions to Manchuria and furnished the Chinese and the North Koreans with arms, military supplies, fuel, foodstuffs, and medicine,[24] and thirteen member nations of the United Nations, which had sent varying numbers of armed men and medical units on the South Korean side. Casualties on both sides were enormous, and the entire peninsula was reduced to rubble. Communist leaders were later to report that some 600,000 private dwellings, 8,700 factories, 5,500 schools, and 1,000 hospitals or clinics in North Korea had been destroyed as a result of the war, the great bulk of them in 1950 or 1951.[25] Facilities for electrical power, transport, and irrigation had also been destroyed.

The war, particularly during the stage when the North Korean forces were compelled to retreat to the north in the face of concerted counterattack by the South Korean and American forces, had also exposed the weaknesses of the North Korean political structure so carefully built up since 1945. A large portion of the population collaborated with the enemy while they were in control of various parts of North Korea, and a great number of North Koreans chose to flee to South Korea when the allied forces withdrew. The rank and file of the Korean Workers' Party also proved to be filled with "impure elements, cowards, and mixed elements" and the party found it necessary to discipline 450,000 of the 600,000 members between December 1950 and November 1951, expelling many of them from the party.[26] The Korean communists had to start the task of building political and economic structures virtually anew at the end of the war.

Chapter 6

Toward a Party of Kim Il-sŏng

The preparation for the reconstruction of the party began long before the truce was signed at Panmunjom in July 1953. Kim Il-sŏng's speeches at the third plenum of the Central Committee in December 1950, the fourth plenum in November 1951, and the fifth plenum in December 1952 had already set forth the general line which the postwar party would follow. He stressed at the third plenum, during the period of retreat, that the party lacked "steel-like discipline." The party had failed to forge a close bond with the masses because formalistic party propaganda and educational work had failed to penetrate into the masses. The cadres were suffering from bureaucratic mannerisms, and they had not properly engaged in criticisms and self-criticisms. Furthermore, work done in compliance with party directives had not been properly inspected.[1] At the fourth plenum, Kim stressed the need for the party to expand and strengthen into a mass party. Quoting extensively from Lenin and Stalin, he argued that the close bond with the masses was the fountain of "indomitable power of the party." But, according to Kim, party activities had been carried out mechanically, and the masses were not provided with proper propaganda and explanation. With such defects, the party cadres could not understand, organize, or mobilize the masses. Instead, the cadres were only issuing orders or coercing the masses. He also found the selection and training of the cadres wanting. Particularly he stressed the need to train members of party cells who could effectively provide leadership in raising the level of ideological consciousness of the members.[2]

Kim had also voiced similar criticisms at the fifth plenum. He argued that the role of party organs and party cadres should be enhanced and the party spirit of members heightened. The selection and allocation of cadres, as well as the inspection of works carried out, needed improvement. The bond between the party and the masses needed to be strengthened, and the ideological work—propaganda and education—intensified.[3]

None of these themes were new. As early as August 29, 1946, at the inaugural conference of the North Korean Workers' Party, Kim had characterized the new party as a mass party uniting workers, farmers, and intelligentsia, and stressed the need to forge a close link between the party and the masses. The party was to develop into a "combat unit and the vanguard of the working masses."[4] At the second congress of the party, held in March 1948, he had criticized the cells for their numerous weaknesses, which had led to the situation in which members lacked firm convictions about their responsibilities or activities. Lack of inspection was criticized, and bureaucratism and formalism were listed as principal weaknesses of the cadres. They were engaging in bureaucratism whenever they shouted at, ordered, threatened, or intimidated the people. They were engaging in formalism when they simply adopted innumerable resolutions and guiding principles instead of going to the people.[5]

Kim Il-sŏng's speeches at the fourth and fifth plenums, however, contained new elements that were to have far-reaching implications for the party and certain members of its top hierarchy in the postwar years. This is because the main thrust of his speech at the fourth plenum was an attack against the left-wing error of "a closed-door tendency" or "exclusionism" committed by the Organization Department of the party. What this meant was that the party had refused admission to "those toiling peasants who [were] fighting at the front and in the rear with all their patriotic devotion, for fear of a drop in the proportion of workers, clinging only to the prewar rate of its growth without consideration for the present situation when, owing to the barbarous bombings of the enemy, factories have been destroyed and the number of workers has dwindled sharply."[6] Not only that, but the party had "committed the grave error of trying to settle all matters by means of meting out Party penalties at random."[7] According to Kim, the offense committed by some 80 to 85 percent of all those punished was mishandling (burning, burying, or hiding) party membership cards during the war.[8] This was obviously a prime example of conducting party affairs mechanically.

The "left-wing error," of course, was quickly corrected after Kim's speech, and the membership reached the one million mark by the time the fifth plenum was held in December 1952. The percentage of poor peasants in the membership also rose from 54.7 on July 1, 1950, to 57.4 on November 1, 1952.[9] Obviously party organizations at various levels could not have adequately screened the onrush of new members. Kim stated at the fifth plenum that an "absolute majority" of the 450,000 new members admitted to the party during the war, most of whom were likely to have been admitted between the fourth and fifth plenum, were green both politically and in practical experience, and about half of them could barely read and write the Korean language.[10] Obviously, quality had been downgraded for the sake of quantity.

The significance of these events in the internal politics among the top leaders of the party was that Hŏ Kai-i, vice-chairman of the party and the head of the Organization Department, opposed the open-door policy.[11] An additional point of importance is that Hŏ, a former party functionary in the Tashkent Province of the Soviet Union, was regarded as the leading figure among those dispatched from the Soviet Union after 1945,[12] and he was presumed to have closer ties with the Soviet embassy in Pyongyang than the others. He was also considered to be the principal architect of the new party structure in North Korea.[13] By publicly denouncing such an important figure, Kim Il-sŏng may have been obliquely announcing his independence from Moscow.

The new aspect in Kim's speech at the fifth plenum was his stress on the struggle against liberal tendencies and the remnants of factionalism. His tirade against the factionalists was vehement. He charged that they lacked party spirit and were politically corrupt. Blinded by material privilege, they had estranged themselves from the masses, lost sight of party work and revolutionary tasks, and only sought after their personal interests. They put on airs about their past revolutionary careers, and regarded minor jobs as beneath them "in spite of their inability to tackle big tasks." In addition, they constantly engaged in "unprincipled complaints" and banded together with others who shared an affinity on the basis of being relatives, old friends, or because they came from the same localities. Those who listened to Kim at the plenum could have sensed that a major battle was afoot because he charged that "some leading functionaries of the party" shared these traits.[14]

The party did not have to wait long to find out who the factionalists were. Kim's fifth plenum report served as the basic document in the purge of the group known as "the domestic faction"—those who had been active in the communist movement within Korea before 1945. At the head of this faction, of course, was Pak Hŏn-yŏng, who had emerged as the top leader of the entire communist camp in Korea, both north and south, in 1945. For many months, all party units down to the cell level were ordered to hold discussion meetings, with Kim's report as the basis for criticism and self-criticism. Additional reference materials relating to the "crimes" of the Pak group were prepared, and former South Koreans in particular were required to examine their past relations with Pak in detail, reporting upon events that "substantiated" the charges being made.[15] The charges prepared, the Military Tribunal Department of the Supreme Court, in early August 1953, tried and convicted twelve high-ranking party cadres of South Korean origin, some of them the closest associates of Pak Hŏn-yŏng. While Pak himself was not named a defendant, his name was mentioned often in connection with various criminal acts. The charge against the Pak clique was that they had been employed as spies by American imperialists. Their alleged intent had been to "establish a colonial and capitalist regime under the control of the American imperialists." For this high treason, ten were sentenced to death, one was sentenced to sixty years in prison, and the other to thirty-three years.[16] For some reason, Pak was not tried until December 1955, when he was also sentenced to death.[17]

The struggle against factionalists, however, did not end with the elimination of these leaders. The party carried out numerous later campaigns to "root out the remnants of factionalist thought." This practice of purifying the thoughts of any and all that might have been contaminated by the "evil" character of the accused is not unique to Korea. John Gittings, in analyzing the developments in China, has also concluded:

> Once the dismissal of a particular leader has been decided upon, meetings are held from Central Committee level downwards at which all those present are obliged to scrutinize their relationship with the accused and to "expose his crimes." The charge sheet which eventually emerges may have little to do with the actual offences which led to his dismissal. The whole process is further encouraged by the importance always attached to rewriting the historical record in Communist China (and for that matter in dynastic China).[18]

While the party was engaged in the struggle against the factionalists, it had concurrently pushed the Three-Year Economic Development Plan (1954–1956) designed to rehabilitate completely all branches of the national economy from war damage and attain the prewar level of industrial and agricultural production. The emphasis has been placed on heavy industry, and the arduous task of reconstruction was relentlessly pursued. By August 1956, the party announced that each industrial field had overfulfilled its quota.[19] Between 1957 and 1961, the party was to implement the First Five-Year Plan, which was to "build the foundations of socialism" in North Korea.

In the political arena, the party leadership appears to have been engaged in intensive review of the current state of the party. In spite of repeated exhortations, party members continued to display weaknesses that inhibited progress in both economic and political fields. Having eliminated the most formidable opponents from the party's leading positions and having cleared the party of their principal underlings, Kim Il-sŏng evidently decided to launch a movement to rebuild the party in a new mold, or to engage in a concerted effort to strengthen the party organization. This can be seen from the fact that Kim Il-sŏng, the chairman of the party, delivered no less than three long speeches at the Central Committee plenum held between April 1 and 4, 1955, all of which were devoted to party affairs. The two speeches delivered on the opening day were entitled, respectively, "On Further Intensifying the Class Education of the Party Members" and "On Eliminating Bureaucratism." The concluding speech of the plenum on April 4 was entitled "On Some Questions of Party and State Work in the Present Stage of the Socialist Revolution." In addition, the party issued in the same month (without giving the specific date of issue) "Theses on the Character and Tasks of Our Revolution." Since these "theses" were included in subsequent editions of Kim Il-sŏng's writings, we can presume that they were also authored by the chairman. Obviously the chairman was intent on impressing the party members that the party had reached a turning point, and that more earnest efforts were about to be made for the purpose of eradicating past weaknesses and solidifying the party.

These theses necessarily dealt with more general principles.[20] They declared that "all the tasks of the anti-imperialist and anti-feudal democratic revolution were fulfilled in the northern half (of Korea) and its people [had] gradually entered the period of transition to socialism." The basic task of the revolution at the current stage was defined as that of overthrowing "the aggressive forces of U.S. imperialism and their ushers and allies" and to free the people in South Korea "from imperialist and feudal oppression and exploitation . . . thereby achieving the country's reunification along democratic lines and attaining complete national independence."[21]

The theses then expounded the need to strengthen the North Korean economy, stressing the need to "develop the productive forces of industry and agriculture." It is noteworthy that the theses also referred to "the individual peasant economy predominant in the countryside" as a "big obstacle to the speedy rehabilitation and future development of agriculture." "Without transforming the peasant economy and individual trade and industry along socialist lines," it declared, "it is impossible to ensure the development of the productive forces, radically improve the people's livelihood," and so on.[22] Clearly, the party had decided that individual farming would soon end, and a collective system would be introduced. The North Korean farmers were collectivized into 3,843 cooperatives by 1958.

In his speech on class education, delivered on April 1, Kim Il-sŏng was more specific on the weaknesses among the party members as well as their cures. While the same defects had been pointed out on numerous occasions before, the speeches of April 1 are notable for their provision for practical and specific methods of work or the correct style of work. To be sure, many of the points made by Kim in 1955 had been made before by Lenin, Stalin, Georgi Dimitrov, and Mao Tse-tung,[23] but at least in the North Korean context, what Kim said was new.

The "manifestations" which Kim Il-sŏng found to be "detrimental to the interests of revolution" in his speech on class education were as follows. (1) Some of the party members lacked a correct understanding of the character and fundamental tasks of the Korean revolution. They lacked conviction concerning the cause of reunification and independence of the country; in particular, they had only a vague idea of the prospects of the revolution. (2) Some of the members attached more weight to their personal interests than to the interests of the revolution, the party, and the people. (3) Some party members were not waging a principled struggle against exploitative practices, had not rid themselves of the obsolete bourgeois viewpoint toward labor, and took a dishonest attitude toward state and public property. (4) Some party members and "responsible cadres," blinded by careerism and avarice, persisted in "such bureaucratic work methods as glossing over facts and flattering their superiors, while blustering at their subordinates." (5) Some party members still engaged in "the evil factional practices." Lastly, (6) some party members and cadres, carried away by successes, became indolent and did not sharpen their vigilance against the enemy.

To eradicate these defects, Kim Il-sŏng prescribed the following remedies. In doing so, he also described the practices of the past, and hence some of the points he made deserve to be quoted at length.

The first remedy he prescribed was that the entire party should study the theory and principles of Marxism-Leninism *by linking them with the specific realities of Korea,* and should conduct the class education of party members in combination *with vigorous everyday work in the country and through practical struggle.* While this dictum may appear to be rudimentary to those familiar with Mao's *On Practice,* in the contest of North Korea in 1955 it was revolutionary. The following quotation from Kim Il-sŏng starkly reveals the situation that prevailed in North Korea:

> We must in no case permit such tendencies as mechanically introducing and instilling into the minds of Party members the fighting experience of the parties of other countries, without studying it in relation to the actual situation in Korea. . . . We study Marxist theory, viewpoints, and methods and the experience of the fraternal parties in their revolutionary struggles in order to analyze accurately the problems of the revolution and political and economic questions in our country and to have a guide in our own struggle.
>
> However, many of our Party members do not critically assimilate the battle experience of the parties of other countries; they swallow it whole. They know how to copy foreign things intact, but not how to apply them properly to the actual conditions of our country. . . .
>
> The political education of our Party members should not be confined to learning Marxist-Leninist theory and advanced experience merely for the sake of knowing them; instead, the emphasis should be laid on learning how to apply them properly.[24]

The second proposed remedy reflected the low level of ideological knowledge and training among party members. Kim argued that party members should be educated in Marxism-Leninism so that they could "establish a dialectical materialist outlook." They should be instilled with "a clear idea of the general laws governing the development of nature and society" and "the scientific knowledge about the essence of class struggle." They must be taught to "maintain a high sense of honor and pride" and foster in them "revolutionary optimism based on a firm belief in the emancipation of the oppressed working people and the inevitable victory of socialism and communism."

The third point in Kim's speech was that party members should be trained to become "indomitable revolutionary fighters and ardent political workers" who would sacrifice even their lives, subordinate their own wishes, value labor, and be able to discern class enemies. Criticism and self-criticism were to be employed extensively to rectify errors.

Along with these changes and reemphasis in the content of political education, Kim Il-sŏng, as mentioned earlier, called for "a fundamental change" in the methods of political education and study within the party. He charged that the party organizations had so far:

> failed to get rid of such formalistic methods of political education as passing on and cramming the teaching material into the heads of Party members in the manner of reading a Talmudic service, according to one and the same study program, without concretely taking into account the knowledge and political and theoretical level of individual Party members.
>
> In Party study, emphasis has been laid on merely memorizing or citing unnecessary dates, phrases, and theses, while making little effort to grasp essential ideas or political content. As a result, Party study has failed to provide [them with] a living knowledge which can be of help in practical life, nor has it been helpful in elevating their class consciousness.
>
> Furthermore, some propaganda workers in charge of Party education fail to give their explanations in plain and simple language . . . but reel off difficult terms and theses which they themselves do not fully understand. In many cases, our press carries poor and extremely tedious propaganda articles and comments under headings which all sound more or less the same.[25]

In order to overcome these defects, the premier ordered that the educational system at all levels and all teaching materials should be revised. The party press was ordered to improve its articles "both in form and content so that the masses at large can understand them easily and find them interesting." Party organizations at all levels were also ordered to regard ideological education "as the most important task of Party organizations" and to link the party's political work with economic work. Kim's denunciation of "a number of our Party organizations and leading cadres" was harsh: "[They] have become petty routineers . . . , they do little to keep up daily contact with the masses, addicting themselves only to shock campaigns, are out of touch with actual conditions [at the grassroots level] and fail to see important problems of Party policy."[26]

The correct style of work received more attention in Kim's second speech, delivered on April 1. In fact, the entire speech, entitled "On Eliminating Bureaucratism," was devoted to this subject.[27] According to Premier Kim, the methods of party leadership and the cadres' style of work was especially important because the party needed to mobilize and organize the broad masses of the people. "When the Party's line and policies are correct and proper measures are adopted for their implementation," according to the premier, success in work depended on what methods the functionaries employ in actual work, on how they organize and mobilize the masses to do the work. But the premier found a "harmful and anti-popular style of work . . . in various forms within the Party and government bodies, high and low."[28] Examples were army officers acting like old-time commanding officers, "interior servicemen" (policemen) acting like old-time policemen, and state functionaries assuming the airs of old-time officials, while party workers were showing off the party's authority.[29] Many of the high-level personnel were conceited and performed their work in a formalistic way or just skimped on it, sticking to their own subjective views. Many lower-level personnel engaged in flattery and blindly followed the instructions of their superiors. The premier, therefore, called for better selection, education, and guidance of party and state personnel, better class education, and the strengthening of collective leadership and inner-party democracy. Through these means, the party and state personnel were to be taught to understand that "the revolution is a struggle of the masses and this struggle is aimed solely at the emancipation and welfare of the masses of the people, and that the Party can carry out the revolution only by relying on the masses of the people."[30]

Further, the party was told to breathe the same air as the masses, and by safeguarding their interests, rally them around the party and the government.[31] The elimination of bureaucratism, therefore, was the most important step in forging a bond between the party and the people. The premier had made these points nine years ago, in July 1946, but obviously his exhortations had not been heeded properly. This probably explains why his criticisms were more pointed than before. Even though he refrained from mentioning names, his references to the various kinds of errors committed by cadres at various levels were obviously meant to warn the indolent. By emphasizing similar themes twice on the same day at an important plenum of the Central Committee, he obviously intended to bring a decisive turnabout in the cadres' attitude. Indeed, the premier was to mention many of these points again in his concluding speech of April 4. An additional point introduced on the last day of the plenum was the premier's instruction to high officials to "go down to the lower levels and stay there for a long period to assist their functionaries in their actual work."[32] A similar practice in China was labeled the "hsia-fang" (downward) movement.

In essence, the premier's principal concern in 1955 was to change the behavior patterns of party and state personnel. In earlier times, it is clear that the instructions provided by the party had remained largely as formal knowledge ("rote memory") and had made little impact on the behavior of party personnel, who persisted in their formalistic, ritualistic, and bureaucratic behavior, which elicited hostile and indifferent reactions from the masses. The premier was therefore urging party members to internalize the knowledge gained, in order to change their attitudes and behavior. Theory or knowledge had remained on a separate plane from practice; now these needed to be fused.

Another important thrust of the premier's speeches was the need to domesticate communism. Given the history of communism in Korea, it was quite understandable that Korean communists should mechanically introduce abstract tenets of Marxism and Leninism as well as the experience of the more successful parties abroad. The Korean communists had generally lacked the sophistication, experience, and confidence to relate the abstract theories and foreign experiences to the realities in Korea. Even the premier himself had not dared or felt it appropriate to speak out on this subject before 1955. The power and influence of the Communist Party of the Soviet Union (CPSU) had been too great for the Korean communists to strike out on their own. Only with the waning of the predominance of the CPSU in international communism, brought about by the death of Stalin and the rising status of the Chinese Communist Party, along with the growing confidence and maturity of the Korean communists, was it possible for Kim Il-sŏng to move toward the Koreanization of communism.

Kim Il-sŏng took a more decisive step toward Koreanization at the end of the same year, on December 28, 1955. The title of the speech he delivered at a conference of party propagandists and agitators—"On Eliminating Dogmatism and Formalism and Establishing Chuch'e in

Ideological Work," reflects his principal concern.[33] The main thrust of the speech was on establishing *chuch'e*, or "the foundation of action." Lacking a firm foundation or criteria of action, according to the premier, the Korean communists inevitably engaged in dogmatism and formalism and blindly followed the policies of others. While the premier had alluded to this problem in April, he was intent on delineating the essence of "the foundation of action" in his December speech.

The promotion of the Korean revolution, of course, was to be the principal criterion of action, as Kim Il-sŏng himself had stated in April. But how could the Korean communists identify themselves with the tasks of the Korean revolution and establish a correct "foundation of action"?

Kim answered these abstract questions by outlining the strategies he was to follow in later years. They were, first, the removal of Russian influence, represented by the Russian-Koreans in the high echelons of the party, and second, the exaltation of the experiences of the anti-Japanese guerrillas in Manchuria. Henceforth, the experiences of the Manchurian guerrillas, described in Chapter Three, were to be exalted as the crystallization of everything desirable—including *chuch'e*, the mass line, and the "party character." Thus Kim's December speech was a blueprint for the future of the Korean Workers' Party.

The premier's denunciation of Russian influence was unmistakable. His sharpest attack was directed against Pak Ch'ang-ok, the Russian-Korean, who was concurrently Vice Premier and head of the National Planning Commission in the government and Vice-Chairman of the Central Committee and the chief of the Propaganda Department of the party.[34] Because of Pak's latter position, all the criticisms directed against the propagandists and agitators in the party could be read as being aimed at him. These criticisms were that they did not know the history, geography, and the customs of the Korean people; even though the fifth plenum of the Central Committee had decided to actively publicize the history of the Korean people's struggle and its "valuable cultural heritage," the "workers in the field of propaganda failed to do [this]. They went so far as to forbid the newspapers to carry articles on the anti-Japanese struggle of the Korean people."[35] Lectures on Korean history were neglected even in schools; in the People's Army vacation home, there were the pictures of the Siberian steppes but none of Korean scenery; in the local "democratic publicity halls," there were diagrams illustrating the Soviet Union's Five-Year Plan but not a single diagram illustrating the Three-Year Plan in North Korea; in the primary schools, there were the portraits of Mayakovsky and Pushkin but none of Koreans. Materials for schoolbooks were drawn exclusively from foreign works, never from Korean works.[36] The KWP's daily organ, *Nodong Sinmun*, mechanically copied the headlines of *Pravda*.[37]

Another party leader singled out by the premier was Pak Yŏng-bin, a man from Tashkent who had headed the Organization Department of the party since 1953. Having recently returned from his trip to the Soviet Union, Pak allegedly advocated that the Korean communists eliminate slogans denouncing American imperialism because the Soviet Union was taking the line of reducing tension in the international arena. But, according to Kim Il-sŏng, such an assertion had nothing to do with revolutionary initiative:

> It is utterly ridiculous to think that our people's struggle against the U.S. imperialists conflicts with the efforts of the Soviet people to ease international tension. Our people's condemnation and struggle against the aggressive policy of the U.S. imperialists toward Korea are not contradictory, but conducive to the struggle of people of the world for lessening international tension and for defending peace.[38]

It should be noted in passing that the above paragraph hints at a probable source of conflict between the Korean and Soviet communists at this time. It is quite possible that the North Korean communists were irritated by Premier Khrushchev's policy of peaceful coexistence with the United States, which was regarded as the arch enemy of the Korean communists. It is also possible that the North Koreans decided to stress *chuch'e* at this time because of such policy differences. It is significant that Kim Il-sŏng referred to the current Chinese rectification campaign in his December speech. He said: "We must establish a strong educational policy for the entire party. There is a need [in a party] to conduct a rectification [campaign], as in the Chinese party. Rectification is none other than forging of party character [tang-sŏng] and thought education."[39]

It is possible that the premier not only found the rectification campaign in China worthy of copying, but also shared the Chinese concern that the CPSU was abandoning its struggle against American imperialism. Thus, the changing atmosphere within the international communist camp definitely constituted one of the factors contributing toward Premier Kim's turn toward nationalism.[40] Kim's December speech was directed not only toward the members of his party but also toward his allies abroad.

It is interesting, and to some extent significant, that Kim Il-sŏng introduced the theme of respecting "revolutionary fighters," a theme that was to become an obsession of the party during the next decade or more, in connection with establishing *chuch'e*. He asserted that because of the lack of *chuch'e*, "many comrades" did not respect "our revolutionaries." Until recently, according to the premier, "more than 100 comrades" who had taken part in revolutionary struggles in the past were "buried in obscurity"; now, however, they were attending the Central Party School. He had placed many other former revolutionaries in the Ministry of the Interior, but several of them were dismissed on grounds of incompetence. The same ministry had the audacity to keep a former comrade of Kim's as the county police chief for eight years. "This is quite an improper attitude toward revolutionaries," Kim asserted. Obviously he was intent on correcting the situation.

Kim also launched the "learn from the guerrillas" movement in the same speech. His instruction was specific. He said, "All party members have to learn from the attitude of the guerrillas toward the masses."[41] He argued that the anti-Japanese guerrillas had been able to hold out for so long against a formidable Japanese armed force "because the guerrillas had the correct mass viewpoint and the support of the masses." The masses supported and protected the guerrillas because the guerrillas "had always defended their interests and fought for them at the risk of our own lives."[42] Subsequently, the party press began to print a seemingly endless number of articles and books about the activities of the guerrillas, all of which exalted the wisdom, bravery, patriotism, and warm-heartedness of their leader, Kim Il-sŏng. Reading and studying the memoirs of the anti-Japanese guerrillas became a daily requirement for all party members, regardless of rank. Clearly, Premier Kim Il-sŏng was intent on domesticating communism, but the model chosen for it was drawn from his own experience.

In spite of the premier's harsh criticisms of Pak Ch'ang-ok and Pak Yŏng-bin, these Russian-Koreans had not been removed from their leadership positions, which may have reflected the continuing sensitivity of the North Koreans toward the CPSU. Kim Il-sŏng also shared his power with some of the returnees from Yenan, notably such leaders as Ch'oe Ch'ang-ik, who had been a vice-premier since 1952, and Kim Tu-bong, who had been the chairman of the Presidium of the Supreme

People's Assembly since its inception in 1948. But a final showdown came in the fall of 1956, in the wake of the de-Stalinization campaign in the Soviet Union that had been launched by Nikita Khrushchev's secret speech at the Twentieth Congress of the CPSU in February.

While the full details of the clash between those for and against Kim Il-sŏng have never been adequately reported in official publications, there can be no doubt that the August and September (1956) plenums of the Central Committee were the scenes of intense drama. An article in the February 1957 issue of the party's theoretical journal *Kŭlloja* (The Worker), for example, asserted that contrary to the arguments of "anti-Party factionalists" such as Ch'oe Ch'ang-ik, Pak Ch'ang-ok, Yun Kong-hŭm, Sŏ Hwi, Yi P'il-gyu, and others—men who "were crushed in the August and September plenums of last year"—the economic policies of the government had been "consistently correct," both in the past and in the present.[43] The lead article of the July issue of the same journal again cited the same culprits, with the addition of Kim Sŭng-hwa, and asserted that they had attempted to subvert the unity of the party by "babbling about so-called freedom and the expansion of democracy, just as was done in bourgeois propaganda." The real purpose of their slogans "freedom" and "democracy" was to turn the party into "a factionalist clique of pedagogues."[44] In November 1957, Kim Il-sŏng himself referred to Ch'oe Ch'ang-ik and his group as "traitors of the revolution and extremely corrupt elements" whose "conspiracy was so extremely sinister that had it not been uncovered and crushed in time, it might have brought grave consequences to our party and our revolution."[45] Of those named above, Pak Ch'ang-ok (rank 7 in the Central Committee at the Third Congress of the KWP in April 1956) and Kim Sŭng-hwa (rank 35) were the Russian-Koreans. All the others—Ch'oe (rank 8), Sŏ Hwi (rank 19), Yi P'il-gyu (rank 97), and Yun Kong-hŭm (rank 68)—were of Yenan origin. These official accounts lend credence to a report of a South Korean analyst that some of the leading elements of the Russian and Yenan factions in the KWP leadership attempted to overthrow the one-man dictatorship of Kim Il-sŏng and bring about a major shift in economic policy, away from an emphasis on heavy industry and toward improving the ordinary person's standard of living. But the opposition groups were outnumbered and soundly defeated.[46]

What followed was largely predictable. Party journals launched an intense campaign to discredit the opposition forces. At the same time, the party launched a "concentrated guidance" or inspection campaign in the beginning of 1957, to attack "sectarians" and "sectarian influences" within the party. In large measure, the process involved was identical with the campaign launched in 1953 against Pak Hŏn-yŏng and his cohorts from South Korea. By the time the First Conference of Representatives of the KWP met in March 1958, "problems of party unity and solidarity" seem to have been resolved to the satisfaction of Kim Il-sŏng and his cohorts. All the major rivals of Kim—including Kim Tu-bong, the "titular head of the Yenan group"—were now removed from the scene. While Kim Tu-bong had not been involved in any of the internecine squabbles, Kim Il-sŏng stated in his concluding address before the Conference: "We worked with Kim Tu-bong for ten years. But during those years he nurtured an evil dream. While remaining uncommunicative with us, he opened up his heart only to Han Pin and Ch'oe Ch'ang-ik."[47]

In denouncing his former opponents, the triumphant leader enunciated three political principles that were to serve as future guidelines for the party:

Originality and Individualist Heroism. Why do the factionalists and parochialists behave like this? Because they think they are the smartest men, the cocks of the walk. Kim Tu-bong, too, thought himself the wisest. Thus, he was entirely discontented with the Party, was finding fault with what had been proposed by the Party, and tried to put forward something original himself. . . . All this stems from individualist heroism which is characterized by disloyalty to the Party, careerism, and a thirst for fame.[48]

Technology vs. Party Leadership (Experts vs. Reds). We are also witnessing the wrong tendency among some people to believe in the omnipotence of technique, thinking themselves the greatest authorities in technical matters and refusing to accept the Party's leadership readily. This, too, is a very harmful propensity. What is the use of technology, if it is separated from the will and leadership of the Party?[49]

Proletarian Dictatorship. As long as small commodity producers, private merchants, and manufacturers, even in limited numbers, remain in urban and rural areas, as long as the tasks of the socialist revolution have not yet been accomplished, and, moreover, there exists a regime of landlords and capitalists in the southern half, how can we neglect to consolidate the dictatorship of the proletariat?[50]

Thus, between 1953 and 1958, the KWP was significantly transformed, or at least a beginning had been made to transform it. Before the end of the war, the KWP was largely a copy of the CPSU, not only in terms of its organization and structure but in the style of its operation as well. The superstructure that was created (or imposed, as some of the critics would have it) under the Soviet aegis remained a foreign body and had not rooted itself in the native soil. In spite of a large number of recruits, or because of them, the KWP had remained a hodgepodge of barely literate elements seeking security, status, and power. The resounding defeat of the North Korean Army in the fall and winter of 1950—labeled as a period of "temporary strategic retreat" by the official historians—could not have helped but lower the morale and discipline of the party members and tarnish the prestige of the party in the eyes of the masses. In this situation, it is quite understandable that Kim Il-sŏng and his cohorts decided to rebuild the party by domesticating foreign ideology and organization. It is also logical that the Korean communists strove to find an anchor in Korean nationalism, stressing that the party's aim was to achieve a distinctively Korean revolution.

It was probably no accident that Kim Il-sŏng chose to emphasize the anti-bureaucratic style of operation as well as such themes as "mass line" at this time. While Lenin and other Soviet writers had expounded these themes in the initial stages of the Bolshevik revolution, the CPSU had changed significantly under Stalin's rule, becoming a much more bureaucratized and formalized party. The Chinese Communist Party, on the other hand, was still grappling with the problem of expanding its influence over the masses through various campaigns and programs. It is only natural that Kim Il-sŏng looked to China for possible models and lessons. One need not become "pro-Chinese" in order to learn from the experiences of the Chinese. During these years, of course, the KWP had reasons to be particularly intimate with the CCP, even more so than with the CPSU. It was the Chinese party that had sent massive forces of "volunteers" to rescue the Korean communists from certain defeat, while the Russians provided only vocal and material support. It is possible, therefore, that a special affinity between Chinese and Korean communists during these years led the Koreans to study the Chinese experience more closely. There is little doubt, however, that Kim Il-sŏng exercised the choice on his own volition, with an intent to strengthen his own party.

The events of these years also leave no doubt that the KWP had been successfully transformed into the party of a single leader, Kim Il-sŏng. By skillful maneuvers, the potential rivals had been removed, one by one. One must recognize, if not admire, Kim Il-sŏng's Machiavellian (or Stalinist?) genius: he successfully eliminated men with close ties to both the CCP and the CPSU, at a time when his party was heavily dependent upon the support of these national parties. In any event, by 1958, at the age of forty-six, Kim Il-sŏng had established undisputed control over the Korean Workers' Party and the Democratic People's Republic of Korea. No longer, as in the past, could he be forced to make concessions to his rivals and to foreign parties; he was now in command.

Chapter 7

The Party of Kim Il-sŏng in Transition

By 1958, Premier Kim Il-sŏng had been in the seat of power for over a decade and a half. Although he had enjoyed distinct advantages over his adversaries from the time he and his cohorts returned to Korea in 1945 because of the support he received from the Soviet occupation forces, this had not been an easy period for him. The veterans of the underground communist movement within Korea (the "natives"), for instance, had built a party structure before Kim returned with the Soviet army, and claimed legitimacy for their leadership. Those returning from northwest China (the Yenan faction), on the other hand, had to be given a share of power not only because of their past achievements in China but because of the physical presence in Korea of their patrons and mentors. The Chinese communists dispatched large "volunteer" forces to Korea in October 1950; they were not withdrawn until October 1958. The Soviet-Koreans, on the other hand, had been part of the Soviet system in Russia, and naturally maintained a close relationship with the Soviet occupation authorities between 1945 and 1948 and with the Soviet embassy thereafter. Of course, aside from these intricate internal political problems, the costly war had rendered not only the position of Kim Il-sŏng but the survival of the new state precarious. The de-Stalinization campaign in the Soviet Union and fluctuating political alignments in the international camp in the aftermath of that campaign had also presented problems.

By 1958, however, Kim had successfully parried all internal and external threats. He had outmaneuvered all of his rivals and was now in an unchallenged position to chart the future course of the party according to his will. The rumbles within the international camp also made it easier for him to pursue his own line of policies without fearing interference from either of the super-powers.

As we have seen in the previous chapter, the future policies of the KWP had been delineated by Kim Il-sŏng in the first years after the war ended. The party was to be solidified into a more effective instrument of power by eliminating such defects as bureaucratism, formalism, and factionalism. Ideological education and training were to be intensified among party members to inculcate stronger conviction in the correctness of Marxism-Leninism as well as Korean nationalism. Those of "impure" background and thoughts were to be re-educated or weeded out from the party, and former colleagues of Kim Il-sŏng were to be exalted. Meanwhile the goal of socialist construction was to be relentlessly pursued by continued emphasis on the development of heavy industry as well as improvements in collectivized farms. All these efforts were seen as a preparation for the peaceful unification of Korea to be brought about under communist hegemony.

While the main efforts of the party leadership in subsequent years shifted from one area to another, reflecting changing international and domestic environments, the KWP pursued its goals intensely during the next two decades. It will be appropriate, therefore, to trace and analyze developments after 1958 topically, paying special attention to some of the more salient events.

CREATION OF A NEW REVOLUTIONARY TRADITION

One of the most important tasks undertaken by Kim Il-sŏng after eliminating his rivals from the party's top leadership positions was to define or create a new revolutionary tradition. This was, of course, a matter of great importance; the victorious leader needed to clothe his power with legitimacy. It was necessary to create a belief, indeed a conviction, among party followers that they owed obedience to the leader not only on account of his victory in the intra-party strife but also because his exalted position had been earned by his past accomplishments. Only when such beliefs are internalized by the followers can the leader's authority to command the present and to define the future be legitimized.

It is significant that Kim Il-sŏng delivered his message concerning the new revolutionary tradition on February 8, 1958, the tenth anniversary of the founding of the Korean People's Army. As the leader revealed in his speech that day, there had been disputes among the army leaders on such crucial questions as "to whom the army belonged or what tradition it should properly inherit." As was the case in the party, the army leadership consisted of leaders with diverse backgrounds, and evidently it was not easy to obtain consensus. Only when all the rivals in the party and the army were gone could Kim Il-sŏng settle the questions in his favor. For example, according to Kim Il-sŏng, there were those who argued that the army belonged to the Democratic National United Front, which was an organization of various "democratic" political parties and social organizations. Acceptance of this point of view would make it impossible for the KWP to exercise dominant control over the army, let alone for Kim Il-sŏng to put his personal imprint upon it. Another group of "factionalists" allegedly argued that the army was properly the heir to the peasant movement which took place in Kilju and Myŏngch'ŏn region of the North Hamgyŏng Province. Presumably the advocates of this view were the veterans of the peasant movement commonly known as the "domestic" or "native" faction. Placing emphasis on this movement naturally would not bring much benefit to Kim Il-sŏng and his cohorts.

There was also the question of what weight should be assigned to the experiences of various anti-Japanese armies and groups that had sprung up in Korea, Manchuria, and China after the Japanese takeover of Korea began in 1905. Immediately after the Japanese forced the old Korean army to disband in 1907, numerous Koreans had organized Righteous Armies and engaged in guerrilla warfare against the Japanese. After 1919, in the wake of nationwide mass demonstrations, exiles in Manchuria had organized Korean Independence Armies to attack the Japanese armed forces in Korea, Manchuria, and Siberia. Some of these nationalists persisted in their efforts in the Manchurian hinterland until the late 1930s. Another small group of men to gain recognition was the Righteous Fighters' Corps (Uiyŏldan) under Kim Won-bong, who had stood on the fringe of the communist movement directing a series of terrorist activities against Japanese personnel and buildings in and out of Korea since 1919. Some of his men had been trained by the Chinese Nationalist government as army officers. Many of them had been dispatched to Korea for secret operations; others had joined the military unit organized in northwest China under CCP aegis in 1941. Lastly, a decision had to be made on the significance of the accomplishments of the Korean Volunteers Corps (later the Korean Volunteer Army) that had been nurtured by the CCP in northwest China. This group, later known as the Yenan faction, had made some contribution to the anti-Japanese military efforts by the Chinese communists before the Japanese capitulation, and they had contributed more significantly to the communist victory over the KMT between 1945 and 1949. Many army divisions in North Korea consisted of these veterans who returned to Korea after the CCP had won its war in Manchuria.[1]

The existence of these several "traditions" and the presence of many veterans from these groups in the new army had made it necessary at first for Kim Il-sŏng to speak of the anti-Japanese tradition in very general terms. In his speech of February 8, 1948, when the Korean People's Army was founded, Kim stated:

> Another specific feature of our People's Army is that it has been formed with the true patriots of Korea as its backbone, [with men] who devoted everything to the anti-Japanese armed struggle for the liberation of the country and the people in the face of severe Japanese suppression in the past. . . . Our People's Army is created today with these patriotic revolutionaries as its backbone and on the basis of the rich experience accumulated by them during the long anti-Japanese armed struggle.[2]

In his 1958 speech, Kim Il-sŏng specifically rejected all the groups other than the Manchurian guerrillas as predecessors of the Korean People's Army, either because they had defended the interests of the propertied classes, or had not developed into military movements, or had not engaged in actual combat. It is noteworthy that Kim cited the Korean Independence League of Yenan but not the Korean Volunteer Army, which was an armed detachment of the League and had participated in anti-Japanese warfare. Kim's position was clear in 1958: "Our People's Army is an army that has inherited the revolutionary traditions of the Anti-Japanese Guerrilla Army [of Manchuria] which, guided by Marxist-Leninist ideas, fought against imperialism in the interests of the workers, peasants, and other working people."[3]

What does inheriting the revolutionary tradition of the anti-Japanese guerrillas mean? "We mean," Kim explained, "that it inherits the ideological system of the Anti-Japanese Guerrilla Army, and its fine method and style of work." In short, the People's Army was to become a replica of what the Manchurian guerrillas were like. What were the guerrillas like, then? Kim Il-sŏng answered this question by projecting the ideals he had put forth since the end of the Korean war:

> The anti-Japanese guerrillas established the traditions of a fighting spirit, in which they fought . . . for the good of the working people, and always lived among the people and struggled hand in hand with the people. The ideas of the Anti-Japanese Guerrilla Army were Marxist-Leninist ideas and its aim was to fight for the establishment of a people's power which would oppose imperialism and safeguard the interests of the working people.
>
> In those days, the guerrillas under the slogan of "As fish cannot live without water, so the guerrilla army cannot live without the people," always loved and respected the people and fought devotedly for the liberation of the fatherland.
>
> The guerrillas were not merely combatants fighting the enemy; they were also propagandists who educated and agitated the people, and organizers who organized and mobilized them.[4]

Premier Kim Il-sŏng thus presented a new model for the Korean People's Army to emulate. He supported this choice by charging that "The anti-Party factionalist elements came out against our People's Army inheriting the revolutionary traditions of the Anti-Japanese Guerrilla Army . . . [because] their aim is to prevent the People's Army from becoming an army with a strong revolutionary spirit like the Anti-Japanese Guerrilla Army."[5] He also charged that the anti-party factionalists either denied that the Korean people had accomplished anything in the anti-Japanese struggle, or unfairly claimed to share credit for the people's achievements. Most likely, Kim was referring to the Soviet-Koreans in the first instance, and the returnees from northwest China in the second instance. In either case, Kim brushed aside these "factionalist" views as "utterly groundless" slander.[6] What this addendum meant was that anyone slighting the "revolutionary tradition" of the Manchurian guerrillas, or paying any attention to the achievements of any group other than the Manchurian guerrillas, would be charged with *lèse majesté*. Thus, through his speech of February 8, 1958, Kim Il-sŏng "established" beyond any doubt that the North Korean Army was to follow his footsteps without deviation. Of course, the directive was not limited to the army. The entire party was to follow the premier's speech verbatim. It was soon revealed that there had been no distinction between the army and the party during the guerrilla era. Kim Il-sŏng was the single leader for both. Kim's words in 1958, therefore, needed to be heeded by both the army and the party.

If there were anyone who still had doubts about the significance of Kim's speech of December 28, 1955, in which he had stressed the need to learn from the guerrillas,[7] his speech of February 8, 1958, left no doubt that he was intent on remolding the party and the army in his image of what the Manchurian guerrillas were like. The veterans of the guerrilla units, who had been ignored or shunned—on grounds of incompetence, according to the premier—were lionized to pen their memoirs, and beginning in 1959, party presses issued volume after volume of their recollections. Between May and October 1959, a team of historians was dispatched to the old battlegrounds of the guerrillas in the Manchurian hills to excavate relevant materials.[8] Historical shrines were erected at Kim's birthplace and many other places mentioned in the annals of Kim's revolutionary struggle. Finally in 1972, a two-block long Museum of Korean Revolution was opened in Pyongyang. Built on a height overlooking the Taedong River, this stone structure comprising 250,000 square meters of space is dedicated solely to glorifying the supreme leader and his family.[9] Histories were rewritten to castigate or ignore all rival movements and to exalt the Manchurian guerrillas.[10]

Among the many themes advanced by the memoirists of the late 1950s and the 1960s, one theme stands out in particular: the wisdom and love of their leader, Kim Il-sŏng. He has been depicted as a person totally dedicated to the cause of patriotism and Marxism-Leninism, and at the same time full of such human qualities as tenderness, compassion, wisdom, acumen, bravery, and perseverance. Once in his proximity, no one could fail to trust him and follow him. Readers are led to believe that Kim had possessed all these qualities even when he was in his early twenties.

In view of the stress placed by the Korean communists on the tradition of the guerrillas and the most outstanding human qualities of Kim Il-sŏng, it might be appropriate to quote a long portion of a typical recollection written by O Paek-yong, one of Kim's followers who subsequently advanced to the rank of general in the army and was appointed vice-chairman of the all-powerful Military Affairs Commission of the Republic. O's recollection, entitled "The First Step in Learning," was featured in a collection of "Recollections of Anti-Japanese Partisans" published in 1959. He wrote:

> There is an old adage that says "the love shown in raising a child is greater than that in giving birth." I believe this is a saying with much truth to it.
>
> But the deep love shown by Marshall Kim Il-sŏng, and his great achievement in leading our people to today's glory, cannot be adequately

expressed in words. Even in the early days of partisan struggle, he poured the deep fountain of love for the fatherland into our hearts, and nurtured the broad perspective of the Marxist-Leninist world view.

I first met Marshall Kim Il-sŏng in 1932, in the early days of organizing the guerrillas at Wangch'ing. Having established the guerrillas in Ant'u, Marshall Kim Il-sŏng came to Wangch'ing and visited our company, platoon, and even the squads who met the guerrillas. He looked after what we ate, what we wore, how we fired our rifles, learned the alphabet, and engaged in political discussions. He has also taught us the way to strengthen our guerrillas organizationally and ideologically.

Even today, I clearly remember his words: "Our guerrilla unit is not only to fight the enemy. We must become communist fighters who realize the people's interests and their ideals. We must become their educators. Among us, however, are those who do not even know the written words we use daily. Without learning, we cannot advance to the great peak of Marxist-Leninist science. Guerrillas must learn while fighting. We must first learn our written words."

The fact was that there were many in our company who could not even write their own names. I was nineteen then, but having been raised in a very poor family, I had not learned our letters (or phonetic symbols).

Having heard Marshall Kim Il-sŏng's words, I was most ashamed that I had no learning. So, I firmly resolved to learn. On the other hand, however, I began to worry. How could I learn Marxism-Leninism, which was said to be difficult to master even in the universities those days. How could a fellow who was completely without learning at such an age master it? At what leisure after fighting the enemy? Even if I had the time, how could I get the paper and pencil in a place where nothing but rocks and trees exist?

Seeing us in this situation, Marshall Kim Il-sŏng told us that one did not have to have money or have to go to school to learn. Then he distributed booklets to our troops and brought some notebooks to us. As was the case for most others there, this was the first time in my life that I had owned a book or a notebook. What moved me more, however, was the fact that he wrote my name, O Paek-yong, on the front of the notebook.

When I opened the notebook, I saw that he had clearly written all the Korean letters and the ten arabic numerals on the first page.

I began to learn the letters he had written as soon as I received the notebook, and with trembling heart, I began to practice writing my name.

He gave me clothing and shoes when I had never bought a new pair of shoes or worn a good pair. I had walked barefoot over the rocky roads and thorny bushes. He gave me weapons to fight the enemy. He gave me a book and a notebook to learn so that I could become a revolutionary. Not only that, but he personally wrote my name on the notebook. I could never forget his great thoughtfulness.[11]

Thus, he is depicted as a fatherly figure who took pains to care for the welfare of his subordinates in every detail in order to promote revolution. The same theme, with varying details, was expounded countless times by every veteran—including former seamstresses for the guerrillas—who had been a part of the movement.

THE CULT OF PERSONALITY

The new revolutionary tradition thus served as a background for building a heightened cult of personality around Kim Il-sŏng. Even before the rival factions were finally eliminated in 1958, Kim had become an object of singular praise and adoration in North Korea, and indeed this matter had become a subject of dispute in 1956 in the aftermath of the de-Stalinization campaign in the Soviet Union, but a new and intense campaign to establish a cult of personality was launched after 1959. The adulation accorded him went to extremes.

Anything meritorious or praiseworthy is attributed to the genius of his generous guidance. He is presented as the personification of all that is good and noble: dedication to the cause of national revolution, commitment to work and progress, complete selflessness, solicitude for the welfare of others, patience, revolutionary optimism, valiant fighting spirit, and implacable hatred of the enemy. No one else, of course, could be like him. But he is clearly presented as an example to emulate. Every factory, farm, school, or kindergarten has a room set aside for Kim's cult. Every spot where the supreme leader stood or sat while giving "on-the-spot guidance" was enshrined as an honored site.[12]

THE CULT OF KIM IL-SŎNG'S FAMILY AND ITS POLITICAL SIGNIFICANCE

Of course, Kim Il-sŏng was not the first communist leader to build a cult around himself. Lenin, Stalin, and Mao Tse-tung found the practice useful in building strong political institutions around them. It is much easier to cultivate loyalties toward a personality than toward new institutions. But the North Korean leader added another dimension to the cult by deifying not only himself but also his family.

The logic behind the deification of Kim's family is a simple one. How could such a unique figure emerge on the Korean scene unless there was an exemplary family behind him? North Korean historians were therefore mobilized to trace Kim's family tree to find patriotic ancestors. They easily discovered that both of Kim's parents were indomitable patriots. They also discovered that one of his uncles had been sentenced to a fifteen and a half year prison term by the Japanese for engaging in patriotic activities and eventually died in prison. One of Kim's younger brothers was found to have been killed by the Japanese for a similar reason when he was only twenty years old. The historians also discovered that Kim's great-great-grandfather (four generations removed), who had originally settled in Kim's birthplace not far from Pyongyang, had led an attack against an "American imperialist ship" S.S. General Sherman, which had violated Korean territory in the summer of 1866. The American merchant ship with a British missionary on board had attempted to force the Koreans to open their ports to trade. Having defied orders to leave, and having caused some casualties among the Koreans, the ship was finally burned by Korean attackers. While it is highly unlikely that any records about the multitude of men employed to attack the foreign ship exist, the North Korean historians were able to find Kim's ancestor among the attackers. In any event, numerous books and articles have been published in North Korea since 1968 to extol Kim's family as the Revolutionary Family. Kim's mother, Kang Pan-sŏk, has been designated as the Mother of Korea.[13]

Was the deification of his family simply an extension of the intense campaign to deify the supreme leader? Or was there any practical political significance to the fact that Kim Il-sŏng's family has been exalted out of all proportion? Outside observers began to ask these questions as the North Korean propagandists relentlessly continued their campaigns on behalf of both the leader and his family.

It was natural, therefore, that observers began to pay special attention to the meteoric rise of Kim Yŏng-ju, the only surviving younger brother of the supreme leader. A man born in 1921, he is reputed to have participated in the guerrilla movement in Manchuria with his brother as a member of the "boys' unit," but he was too young to be of any consequence before and during the Korean War. He had, in fact, been sent to the Soviet Union for university and party education in 1945, and had remained there until 1952. Upon returning to Korea in 1953, he was assigned to the Organization Department of the party's Central Committee.

His family ties obviously helped his career, and by September 1960 he was appointed head of the Organization and Guidance Department of the party, a position of great importance which has been held by the first vice-chairman of the party on previous occasions.

In spite of his functional importance, however, he was given a rank order of 41 at the Fourth Congress of the KWP held in October 1961 which elected eighty-five full members and fifty candidate members.

In October 1966, when the Second Party Conference was held and the party leadership organs were reorganized, Kim Yŏng-ju was appointed a candidate member of the Political Committee and member of the newly established ten-member secretariat, an obvious promotion for a thirty-five-year-old man. He was, however, to rise even further. At the Fifth Congress of the party held in November 1970, the clarion call was clearly audible. Kim Yŏng-ju was promoted to rank order number 6 in the Central Committee and full membership in the Political Committee, which had ten other full members and four alternate members. He was also appointed fourth highest-ranking member in the Secretariat. No one could ignore these signs: the young man was obviously being groomed to succeed to the mantle of power. The intense propaganda about the Revolutionary Family could now be seen to have a practical significance beyond the need to deify the supreme leader.

The supposition that Kim Yŏng-ju was being groomed for succession, however, was subjected to question in December 1972 after the Supreme People's Assembly adopted a new constitution and elected members of the Central People's Committee (CPC) according to new constitutional provisions. As expected, Kim Yŏng-ju was voted into the CPC, "the highest leadership organ of sovereignty of the DPRK," but, curiously enough, his name was listed after two military generals, whose rank order in the KWP were numbers 7 and 8, respectively. As noted earlier, Kim Yŏng-ju's rank order was number 6. There were also reports to the effect that he was suffering from "toxic neurasthenia" (mental depression), and since late 1972, his public appearances had become very irregular; he has disappeared from public view for months at a time. These events gave rise to the speculation that all was not well with Kim Yŏng-ju. In February 1974, he was given an assignment as vice-premier in the cabinet, his first venture into government administration.[14]

Doubts about Kim Yŏng-ju's future as the successor to his brother's mantle were intensified when rumors began to reach Japan—through pro-DPRK Korean travelers from Japan—that Kim Il-sŏng's son, Kim Chŏng-il, was being groomed as the successor. These travelers referred to Kim Chŏng-il in 1973 simply as an important personality in North

Korea.[15] South Korean sources then began to refer to him as the successor, with reports that he was appointed head of the Culture and Art Department of the party in 1970 and promoted to the post of secretary of the party in charge of organization and propaganda, and concurrently made a candidate member of the Political Committee, in September 1973.[16] A South Korean source also reported that Kim Chŏng-il was chosen as his father's successor in December 1973 and that he was appointed a full member of the Political Committee in April 1974. He was said to be in charge of all internal operations of the party.[17]

Since the KWP chose not to release any information concerning the young man who was reportedly born in 1941 and graduated from Kim Il-sŏng University in Pyongyang in 1963, there is no way of verifying these allegations. But speculation about Kim Chŏng-il gathered momentum in 1975 when on November 3, 1975, the *Yomiuri Shimbun* of Tokyo printed an account by three reporters who had recently visited North Korea, to the effect that they had seen a large painting (five meters square) on public display in the streets of Wonsan in which the president and his son were depicted on the same scale. They also saw a photograph of the two figures displayed in the city hall of Pyongyang. From what they saw and heard in North Korea, they had no doubts that the president had decided on his son as his successor.[18] On February 22, 1976, the *New York Times* reported an account by its bureau chief in Tokyo, Richard Halloran, that "North Korean sources here, who carefully reflect the party position, say that President Kim largely turned over domestic duties to his son so that he could concentrate on breaking his nation out of diplomatic isolation."

These reports leave little doubt that the North Korean leader does have a son by the name of Kim Chŏng-il and that he is being groomed for some important position in the North Korean political hierarchy. But there is no official confirmation of the report that the young man was placed in charge of both the organization and propaganda operations of the party, or that he is now in control of all the domestic duties. We do not as yet have a confirmation that Kim Yŏng-ju has been relieved of his position as head of the Organization Department of the KWP. Neither has anyone presented a convincing reason why Kim Il-sŏng would pass over all his trusted cohorts and entrust all the important tasks to his son. In spite of rumors that the North Korean leader has been suffering from a malignant tumor on the neck, he kept up a rather rigorous schedule during the summer of 1975, when he visited China, Europe, and Africa. The succession question may not have to be decided upon for some time.

Will Kim Il-sŏng eventually turn over his power to one of his family members? This is a question that must remain unanswered. The intense campaign to deify his family would certainly make such a transition seem possible. But unless the successor is capable of providing the necessary leadership for the vast power structure built by his predecessor, he could not remain in power for very long. Kim Yŏng-ju and Kim Chŏng-il may possess the qualities needed to rule over the party and the government after the present leader's demise; but this is a proposition that cannot be tested until the day when one of them is placed on the pinnacle of power.

POLITICAL STRUCTURE AND TOP PARTY CADRES

Even the supreme leader, of course, could not rule over the party and the government without trusted subordinates. North Korea is a society of 15 million people and the KWP had a membership of 2 million as of 1975.[19] The amount of leadership needed to direct a large military establishment and a totally controlled economy should not be underestimated. Regardless of whom is at the top, North Korea will need a fair number of experienced cadres at every level. Who, then, are the top cadres of North Korea under Kim Il-sŏng? What kind of individuals have been occupying positions in which they advise the leader and oversee the implementation of decisions?

As in the case in every other communist party, the highest organ of the KWP is the party congress. The congresses are convened so infrequently and their membership is so large, however, that they rarely if ever alter decisions reached by the top leadership.[20] The most important function performed by the party congress is perhaps the election of the Central Committee, although the process itself is a perfunctory one. The congresses in effect rubber-stamp a slate of Central Committee members submitted by the top leadership. In North Korea, the Central Committee is required by the party rules (Article 37) to hold its plenary meetings every six months.[21] During the interval the Political Committee elected by the Central Committee directs all the activities of the party in the name of the Party Central Committee (Article 38). Thus, the Political Committee is the ultimate decision-making organ of the party.

The secretariat, on the other hand, implements the decisions of the Political Committee and administers party business. We can, therefore, understand the characteristics of the top cadres in North Korea if we analyze the membership of these institutions.

Table 16 is a list of all the members of the political committees and the secretariats elected at the Fourth and Fifth Congresses (September 1961 and November 1970) and the Second Party Conference held in October 1966, between the two congresses. Based on this list and our information about the individuals involved, we can make some general comments about the top cadres under Kim Il-sŏng.

The first noticeable point is the high rate of turnover in membership. Of the sixteen full and candidate members elected in 1961 only seven survived in 1966; by 1970, only four remained. In other words, 75 percent of the Political Committee (PC) members elected in 1961 had been removed by 1970 even though all fifteen had been elected to their positions in 1961, presumably with the blessing of the supreme leader. Of the twenty PC members elected in 1966, only eight survived in 1970.

If we remove the top three leaders of the Political Committee—Kim Il-sŏng (number 1 in 1961, 1966, and 1970), Ch'oe Yong-gŏn (number 2 throughout), and Kim Il (number 3 throughout)—from our calculation, the turnover rate will appear even more startling. None of the eight full members of the 1961 PC were reelected in 1970. Out of the five candidate members in the 1961 PC, only one (Hyŏn Mu-gwang), was reelected. Included in the casualty list were those who had held rank orders 4 to 15 in 1961 and 4 to 8 and 11 to 15 in 1966.

Even if we compare the committee's membership in 1966 and 1970, we can discern a very high rate of turnover. None of the three members of the Presidium of the Political Committee (PC) in 1966, other than the top three leaders, were reelected to the PC in 1970. Three out of five regular members of the PC also fell from grace. Of the nine candidate members in 1966, only three were reelected to the PC in 1970.

What, then, is the status of the members of the Political Committee in 1977? Are their positions stable? Are they likely to remain in top party positions through the next several years? The information provided in Table 17 sheds some light on these questions.

A glance at Table 18 leaves no doubt that many top leaders of the KWP, the trusted lieutenants of President Kim Il-sŏng, are rapidly retiring from active posts for reasons of old age and health, and the younger men are replacing them. Thus, Ch'oe Yong-gŏn (rank order

TABLE 16

MEMBERS OF THE POLITICAL COMMITTEE OF THE KOREAN WORKERS' PARTY, 1961–1970

Names	4th KWP Cong. 9/61			2nd KWP Conf. 10/66			5th KWP Cong. 11/70		
	Rank[a]	Pol. Com. Status[b]	Other Posts	Rank	Pol. Com. Status	Other Posts	Rank	Pol. Com. Statuts	Other Posts
Kim Il-sŏng	1	M	Ch., CC	1	M.P.	Gen. Sec.	1	M	Gen. Sec.
Ch'oe Yong-gŏn	2	M	V.C., CC	2	M.P.	Sec.	2	M	Sec.
Kim Il	3	M	V.C., CC	3	M.P.	Sec.	3	M	Sec.
Pak Kŭm-ch'ŏl	4	M	V.C., CC	4	M.P.	Sec.			
Kim Ch'ang-man	5	M	V.C., CC						
Yi Hyo-sun	6	M	V.C., CC	5	M.P.	Sec.			
Pak Chŏng-ae (female)	7	M							
Kim Kwang-hyŏp	8	M		6	M.P.	Sec.			
Chŏng Il-yong	9	M							
Nam Il	10	M							
Yi Chong-ok	11	M							
Kim Ik-sŏn	12	Cand.		7	M				
Yi Chu-yŏn	13	Cand.							
Ha Ang-ch'ŏn	14	Cand.							
Han Sang-du	15	Cand.							
Hyon Mu-gwang	44	Cand.					12	Cand.	Sec.
Kim Ch'ang-bong				8	M				
Pak Sŏng-ch'ŏl				9	M		4	M	
Ch'oe Hyŏn				10	M		5	M	
Yi Yŏng-ho				11	M				
Sŏk San				12	Cand.	Sec.			
Hŏ Pong-hak				13	Cand.	Sec.			
Ch'oe Kwang				14	Cand.				
O Chin-u				15	Cand.		7	M	Sec.
Yim Ch'un-ch'u				16	Cand.				
Kim Tong-gyu				17	Cand.		8	M	Sec.
Kim Yŏng-ju				18	Cand.	Sec.	6	M	Sec.
Pak Yong-guk				19	Cand.	Sec.			
Chŏng Kyong-bok				20	Cand.	Sec.			

TABLE 16 (Cont.)

MEMBERS OF THE POLITICAL COMMITTEE OF THE KOREAN WORKERS' PARTY, 1961–1970

Names	*4th KWP Cong. 9/61*			*2nd KWP Conf. 10/66*			*5th KWP Cong. 11/70*		
	Rank[a]	Pol. Com. Status[b]	Other Posts	Rank	Pol. Com. Status	Other Posts	Rank	Pol. Com. Status	Other Posts
Sŏ Ch'ŏl							9	M	
Kim Chung-rin							10	M	Sec.
Han Ik-su							11	M	Sec.
Chŏng Chun-t'aek							13	Cand.	
Yang Hyŏng-sŏp							14	Cand.	Sec.
Kim Man-gum							15	Cand.	

[a]Rank indicates rank order in which the person is listed when the Central Committee membership is announced.

[b]Abbreviations: M — member
Cand. — candidate member
V.C., CC — Vice-Chairman, Central Committee
M.P. — member, presidium of the Political Committee
Sec. — secretary of the Central Committee, KWP

TABLE 17

Members of the Political Committee of the KWP, 1970–1977

Name[a]	Rank in 1970	Age in 1977	Status
Kim Il-sŏng	1	65	
Ch'oe Yong-gŏn	2	(d.)	Did not appear in public after 1974. Died in late 1976 at age 76.
*Kim Il	3	65	Resigned from premiership in 1976 because of ill health. Appointed First Vice-President of the DPRK.
Pak Sŏng-ch'ŏl	4	65	Appointed Premier in 1976.
*Ch'oe Hyŏn	5	70	Born in 1907. Resigned from Defense Minister's post because of ill health. Currently Vice-Chairman of the National Defense Commission.
*Kim Yŏng-ju	6	55	Said to be in ill health, and rarely appears in public. Appointed Vice-Premier in 1974. Younger brother of Kim Il-song.
O Chin-u	7	67	Appointed Defense Minister in 1976.
Kim Tong-gyu	8	62	Appointed Vice-President in 1974. Most active in protocol or ceremonial functions.
*Sŏ Ch'ŏl	9	70	Born in 1907. Former Director of General Pol. Bureau, Korean People's Army. Assigned to the Supreme People's Assembly. Highest ranking Politburo member in the SPA.
*Kim Chung-rin	10	53	Party cadre had been in charge of South Korean affairs.
Han Ik-su	11	59	General of the KPA. Director, Gen. Pol. Bureau, KPA 1970-1973.
Hyŏn Mu-gwang	12	65	Industrial expert.
Chŏng Chun-t'aek	13	(d.)	Died in 1973. Industrial expert.
Yang Hyŏng-sŏp	14	(?)	Expert on ideology and education.
*Kim Man-gum	15	72	Agricultural expert. Believed to have been removed from Vice-Premier's position in 1973.

[a]Asterisk indicates an inactive or retired member.

TABLE 18

New Appointees to the Political Committee, KWP, 1970–1976

Name	Rank in 1970	Year of Appointment	Status	Functional Areas
Yi Kŭn-mo	54	1973	Cand. then full member	Industrial expert; Vice-Premier, 1973
Ch'oe Chae-u	58	1973	Candidate	Industrial expert; Vice-Premier, 1972; Chmn. of National Planning Commission 1972-73
Kang Sŏng-san	65	1973	Candidate	Party functionary
Yŏn Hyŏng-muk	63	1974	Member and Secretary	Party functionary
Yu Chang-sik	28	1974	Candidate and Secretary	Party functionary; foreign aff. expert
Yi Yong-mu	53	1974	Member	Army General; Dir., General Pol. Bureau, KPA, 1973
Kim Yŏng-nam	80	1974	Candidate and Secretary	Party functionary
Chŏn Mun-sŏp	31	1975	Candidate	Army General

2 in 1970) was replaced by Kim Tong-gyu (rank order 8) as the protocol assistant to the president; Kim Il (rank order 3) was replaced by Pak Sŏng-ch'ŏl (rank order 4) as the chief executive officer of the state; Ch'oe Hyọn (rank order 5) was replaced by O Chin-u (rank order 7) as the defense minister. A few others seem to have fallen from grace for one reason or other. The composition of the Political Committee, therefore, is likely to be very different within a few years when the next congress of the party is held. A number of younger men have been appointed to the Political Committee between 1973 and 1975. These new appointees are listed in Table 18.

Thus the composition of the top leadership of the KWP has changed rapidly during the past few years, and given the old age of some of the Political Committee members elected in 1970, the trend is likely to continue during the next few years.

This situation raises the obvious question about Kim Il-sŏng's successor. Who among these men is likely to inherit the mantle of power? Or, is the successor likely to emerge from outside of the Political Committee such as Kim Il-sŏng's son, Kim Chŏng-il? How is the successor going to be chosen? What role will Kim Il-sŏng play in the choice of his successor? Who wields more influence and power among the top elite? These are very intriguing and important questions, but information about high level politics in North Korea is so scarce that it will be meaningless to offer predictions or guesses. One is reminded of the recent efforts of Western scholars and journalists to predict the pattern of transfer of power in China after the death of Chairman Mao Tse-tung. Even though the Westerners were far more familiar with the political scene in China than in North Korea, virtually no one had anticipated Hua Kuo-feng to succeed to the chairman's post.

Judging from the composition of the Political Committee of the KWP in the mid-1970s, however, one can be reasonably certain that whoever succeeds to the top post in the DPRK is likely to share the basic outlook of President Kim Il-sŏng and will not alter the aims pursued by the KWP during the past two decades. Of course, that KWP's strategies and tactics on such policy areas as unification, economic development, and diplomacy can change depending upon internal and external exigencies. There were indications in 1976 that the party's top leaders were reassessing their past strategies on all these areas.

As in the case in other communist countries, members of the party's Political Committee concurrently occupy key government and army posts. Table 19 indicates the non-party positions held by the PC members. It should be noted here that the Central People's Committee (CPC) in Table 19 is an institution created in 1972 as the "highest leadership organ of sovereignty of the DPRK." The CPC is headed by the president and consists of vice-presidents, a secretary, and other members. At present there is a total of twenty-one members. Four CPC members have died since their appointments in 1972. Only five members of the CPC are currently not members of the party's Political Committee, and it will not be surprising to see these men elected as Political Committee members in the future. One member of the CPC, Vice President Kang Ryang-uk, is not a member of the KWP.

Thus the members of the Political Committee occupy such key posts as the presidency and vice-presidency of the DPRK (two of the three vice-presidents) and the premiership. In addition, five top posts in the military establishments and four key positions in economy are occupied by PC members. Those classified as general functionaries of the party also have expertise in such fields as ideology and education or foreign affairs. The Political Committee as a whole, therefore, is in a position to provide direct leadership to all spheres of governmental activity.

TABLE 19

GOVERNMENTAL POSITIONS HELD BY MEMBERS OF THE POLITICAL COMMITTEE OF THE KWP, 1976

Name	KWP CC Rank in 1970	Pol. Comm. Status[a]	KWP Secretariat	Central People's Comm. DPRK	Other Positions
Kim Il-sŏng	1	M	Gen. Sec.	Pres.	Commander in chief, Korean People's Army; Chairman, National Defense Commission
Ch'oe Yong-gŏn	2	M	Sec.	V. Pres.	Died in late 1976.
Kim Il	3	M	Sec.	V. Pres.	
Pak Song-ch'ol	4	M			Premier (1976-)
Ch'oe Hyŏn	5	M		M	Vice-Chairman, Nat'l Defense Comm.; Army general
Kim Yŏng-ju	6	M	Sec.	M	Vice-Premier (1974-)
O Chin-u	7	M	Sec.	M	Minister of Defense (1976) Army general, Vice-Chairman, Nat'l Defense Comm.
Kim Tong-gyu	8	M	Sec.	V. Pres.	
Sŏ Ch'ŏl	9	M			Vice-Chairman, presidium of the Supreme People's Assembly; Army general
Kim Chung-rin	10	M	Sec.	M	Party functionary (Gen. Bureau on South Korea)
Han Ik-su	11	M	Sec.		Army General
Hyŏn Mu-gwang	12	Cand.	Sec.	M	Chmn., Transp. and Communication Commission
Chŏng Chun-t'aek	13				Died in 1976.
Yang Hyŏng-sŏp	14	M	Sec.	M	Party functionary (ideology and education)
Kim Man-gum	15	Cand.		M	Chmn., Agr. Commission (1972-73)
Yi Kŭn-mo	54	M		M	Vice-Premier (1973-) (industrial expert)
Ch'oe Chae-u	58	Cand.		M	Vice-Premier (1972); Chmn., Nat'l Planning Commission (1972-73)
Kang Sŏng-san	65	Cand.		M	Chmn. Pyongyang City People's Comm. (1973-74) (general party functionary)
Yŏn Hyŏng-muk	63	M.	Sec.	M	Party functionary
Yu Chang-sik	28	Cand.	Sec.	M	Party functionary (foreign affairs expert)

TABLE 19 (Cont.)

GOVERNMENTAL POSITIONS HELD BY MEMBERS OF THE POLITICAL COMMITTEE OF THE KWP, 1976

Name	KWP CC Rank in 1970	Pol. Comm. Status[a]	KWP Secretariat	Central People's Comm. DPRK	Other Positions
Yi Yong-mu	53	M			Army general; Director, Gen. Political Bureau, Korean People's Army (1973-)
Kim Yŏng-nam	80	Cand.	Sec.		Party functionary (general and foreign affairs)
Chŏn Mun-sŏp	31	Cand.			Army general

[a]Abbreviations are for Members, Candidate Member, General Secretary, and Secretary.

Immediately below the Political Committee are the ordinary members of the Central Committee (CC), of which there were 135 (including 50 candidate members) in 1961, and 172 (including 55 candidate members) as of November 1970. These are the individuals who would be called upon by the top leaders at one stage or another to assist in the formation or implementation of key decisions of the party. One's election to the CC is also a clear sign of recognition of dedication, loyalty, and ability by the party and the supreme leader.

One cannot, however, be complacent about his status and power after being elected a Central Committee member. As was the case in the Political Committee, the turnover rate in the Central Committee has been very high. Fifty-four (65 percent) of the eighty-five members of the Fourth CC were not re-elected to the Fifth CC. Of the fifty candidate members of the Fourth CC, twenty-eight (56 percent) were not re-elected to the Fifth CC, fifteen (30 percent) were promoted to full member status, and twelve (24 percent) were retained as candidate members.[22] It is obvious that each member's activities and behavior are closely monitored and scrutinized by his superiors.

What accounts for such a high rate of turnover among the Central Committee members? If we assume that all those elected to the Central Committee in 1961 at the Fourth Congress were uncritically committed to the supreme leader and that there was no political upheaval between the two congresses, we must look for causes other than disloyalty for the turnover. Perhaps a study of the personal characteristics of the CC members would yield some clues.

For purposes of our analysis, Central Committee members were classed into six categories: (1) functionary, general; (2) functionary, economic; (3) technocrat; (4) military; (5) intellectual; and (6) "dignitary." Included in the category of functionary are the career bureaucrats who staff party and state apparatus and are known by the Russians as *apparatchiki*. All those not related to the economic sector are lumped together under the "functionary, general" category. By dignitary we mean the public figureheads or civic personalities who occupy high-sounding positions such as the chairmanship of the presidium of the Supreme People's Assembly or that of the Trade Union Federation, but who are not known to hold much power. The other categories need no elaboration. Of course, not everyone fits neatly into these categories. Some individuals change their career patterns in mid-career. On such occasions, we resorted to the use of hyphens, the first part indicating the earlier pattern.

Using these admittedly crude categories we analyzed those Central Committee members who were promoted within the CC (by receiving higher rank orders), those remaining relatively stable in their rank orders, those removed from the CC altogether, and those newly elected to the Fifth CC.

Those promoted between the Fourth and Fifth CC can be categorized as follows: six general functionary, eight economic functionary, seven military, one military-dignitary, three military-functionary, three dignitary, eight technocrat, one intellectual, and one in a special category, namely, Kim Yŏng-ju. Those remaining relatively stable in their positions with virtually no change in status or with slight demotion in rank order were four general and two economic functionary, three military, one military-dignitary, one military-functionary, and two unknown.

The Fourth CC members not elected to the Fifth CC were: thirty-two general and eleven economic functionary, fifteen military, one military-functionary, six dignitary, two technocrat, six intellectual, and six unknown.

As stated earlier, the Fifth CC introduced 118 new full and candidate members to bring the total to 169. We do have a problem in analyzing the career pattern and inferred specialties of the newcomers because we have no information concerning 38 of the 118 new Central Committee members. These are obviously younger cadres being recruited into the top echelon of the political structure. Our analysis here must therefore be regarded as tentative.

The newcomers to the Fifth CC line up as follows: thirty-nine general and fifteen economic functionary, sixteen military, four dignitary, four intellectual, one special category (Mrs. Kim Il-sŏng), and thirty-eight unknown.

It is rather interesting that in almost every category of leaders the number of newcomers at the Fifth CC closely parallels the number of Fourth CC members not re-elected. It is not likely that this was accidental. One could see the close parallel by comparing columns B and E on Table 20. It is also significant that the proportion of Central Committee members in each category is held almost constant between the Fourth and Fifth CC's, assuming, of course, that the thirty-eight unknown in the Fifth CC are not concentrated in one or two categories. Thus, while there were forty-two general functionary in the Fourth CC (31.8 percent), there were forty-nine in the Fifth CC (28.99 percent). There were twenty-one economic functionary in the Fourth CC (15.9 percent) and twenty-four in the Fifth CC (14.8 percent). The number of military personnel was twenty-five in the Fourth CC (18.9 percent) and twenty-six (15.4 percent) in the Fifth CC. The similarities in other categories can be readily seen by comparing columns A and F in Table 20.

Did any category of cadres suffer more than others? As can be seen from column C of Table 20, the overall casualty rate was 61.4 percent. The highest rate of casualties was suffered by the intellectual (85.7 percent), followed by general functionary (76.2 percent), dignitary (62.5 percent), the military (60.0 percent), and the economic functionary (52.4 percent). The military-turned-functionary had the highest resiliency, with only a 20 percent casualty rate (one out of five) followed by the technocrats, whose casualty rate was 38.5 percent.

The generally high casualty rate would indicate that the supreme leader was not pleased with the overall performance of the party between 1961 and 1970. By the same logic, one might deduce that the supreme leader was least content with the performance of the intellectuals. But the number of individuals involved in that category being so few (only six), one cannot be certain whether he was dissatisfied with the intellectuals as a category in itself or with the particular individuals concerned. On the basis of the data, one cannot also say that the leader was more displeased with the general functionaries (those in the party, state administration, or diplomacy) than the military personnel. The

TABLE 20

MEMBERS OF THE CENTRAL COMMITTEE OF THE KOREAN WORKERS' PARTY FOURTH (1961) and FIFTH (1970) CENTRAL COMMITTEES

	4th CC (A)	Percent	Promoted	Stable	Removed from the 5th CC (B)	Percent of col. (A) (C)	4th CC Mbrs Remaining at 5th CC (D)	Newcomers at 5th CC (E)	5th CC (F)	Percent
Functionaries (general)	42	31.82	6	4	32	76.2	10	39	49	28.99
Functionaries (economic)	21	15.90	8	2	11	52.4	10	15	25	14.79
Military-turned-functionaries	5	3.78	3	1	1	20.0	4	—	4	2.37
Military-turned-dignitaries	2	1.52	1	1	—	0	2	1	3	1.78
Military	25	18.94	7	3	15	60.0	10	16	26	15.38
Dignitaries	8	6.06	3	—	5	62.5	3	4	7	4.14
Technocrats	13	9.85	8	—	5	38.5	8	—	8	4.73
Intellectuals	7	5.30	1	—	6	85.7	1	4	5	2.96
Special category	1	0.75	1	—	—	0	1	1	2	1.18
Unknown	8	6.06	—	2	6	75.0	2	38	40	23.67
Total	132	100.00	38	13	81	61.4	51	118	169	100.00

NOTES: 1. The three top leaders, Kim Il-sŏng, Ch'oe Yong-gŏn, and Kim Il, were excluded from this study.
2. A − B = D; D + E = F.
3. C = B ÷ A

turnover, therefore, must be attributed more to poor individual performance than to any special category of activities.[23]

THE MEMBERSHIP

Below the Political Committee and the Central Committee are the multitude of ordinary members whose number in 1975 was reported to be two million. They have been subjected to constant educational programs, criticisms and self-criticisms, inspections (known as "concentrated guidance" since the mid-1950s), and other means of indoctrination. Those charged with having "impure backgrounds" or "impure thoughts" have been screened out, and presumably only the most loyal, most dedicated, and best trained elements remain in the party. We do not know what proportion of the two million members adequately meet the standards set for them by the party, but the duties required of them by the party rules are awesome indeed.[24]

In spite of the party's constant effort to indoctrinate and improve the entire membership, however, the existence of problems can never be prevented once and for all. Granted that the problem for the party now, in the late 1970s, is not that of loyalty; it is rather that of matching "redness" or ideological faith with expertise and knowledge. This problem was succinctly summed up by Kim Il, the new premier, at the Fifth Congress of the KWP in November 1970:

> There are many cadres among the leading functionaries in state economic organizations and enterprises who come from peasant and worker families and have had very little education. They strive to do a good job and are loyal to the Party, but lack knowledge of the socialist economy and cannot perform economic guidance and business management properly.
>
> Those who have good educations, on the other hand, lack the ability to analyze the economics of the productive activities in their enterprises, although they are well versed in their particular fields.[25]

The nature of the problem confronted by the party can be understood if we look into the generational makeup of the party members. As noted in previous chapters, the KWP had a membership of 1,000,000 by December 1952. By 1961, at the time of the Fourth Party Congress, the membership had reached 1,311,563. This had increased to approximately 1,600,000 in 1965,[26] and then to 2,000,000 in 1975.

The most serious problem for the party lies in the educational quality of the pre-1952 generation, or exactly one-half of the total membership. As is generally known, the educational standard of the Korean people before 1945 was dismally low. Only a few thousand Koreans had managed to attend institutions of higher learning in Japan and Korea before 1945, and only a small proportion of them had studied science, engineerng, or management. Furthermore, since only the relatively rich could afford higher education, most of them were not the kind that would be attracted to communism or acceptable to the KWP. It is safe to assume, therefore, that the educational standard of most of the KWP members before the war was generally low. The problem was aggravated during the war because of a severe attrition of party members, which had required the admission of some 450,000 members between November 1951 and December 1952. As Kim Il-sŏng later revealed, approximately one-half of those who were newly admitted could barely read simple Korean phonetics. All this indicates that some 225,000 members were totally illiterate and that the others were not very well educated.[27]

One must assume, of course, that all the study programs, including adult schools at various levels spread by the party since the war, had their effect. Many of the formerly illiterate members must have advanced their educational levels during the past two and a half decades. But one must remember at the same time that the years after the war were an extraordinarily difficult period for North Koreans, and all of them were required to carry enormous workloads. For many of them, particularly for those who had little opportunity to receive formal education during their childhood, learning would have been a very difficult process. There is, of course, a world of difference between becoming functionally literate and becoming conversant with scientific and technical subjects. Determination or ideological zeal alone sometimes are not sufficient to advance one's intellect.

We have no information as to how many of the prewar and wartime generations are still in the party, or what kinds of rank or position they hold. One would imagine, however, that many of them are still in the party and that most of them hold some sort of cadre position.

These facts are reiterated here because the North Korean leader has been emphasizing the importance of "technical revolution" for some time now. He delivered a long speech on the topic at a Central Committee plenum in August 1960;[28] at the Fifth Congress in 1970, he mentioned it as one of the three building blocks of socialism and communism, the other two being ideological and cultural revolutions.[29] He expounded on the same subject in September 1974 and again in March 1975.[30] What role, if any, can these old cadres play in the technical revolution? Would they not be a hindrance to the party's efforts to modernize North Korean farms and factories?

A suggestion that this was one of the concerns of the party leadership came in the form of Kim Il-sŏng's revelation in September 1974 that "Recently, in particular, the Party center directly sent teams for three revolutions down to factories, enterprises, and cooperative farms to help the workers of lower units, with the result that the ideological, technical, and cultural revolutions are going on successfully." On March 4, 1975, the president gave a more detailed account of the "three-revolution teams."[31]

According to the president, "It is true that the three revolutions can be pushed ahead through the Party organizations since there are Party organizations in all domains and all units of our Party." However, the teams were dispatched directly from the party center to "see to it that the Party organizations and Three-Revolution Teams pushed ahead with the three revolutions by pooling their strength." In others words, the party center was not convinced that party organizations at lower levels were adequately equipped to handle their assigned tasks with sufficient vigor. It is also possible that the ambitious six-year economic development plan, launched in 1971, was not making sufficient headway and that the top leaders decided to spur the workers on by sending these teams from the center. According to the leader, the main purpose of the Three-Revolution Teams was "to lend our cadres good help so they may discard conservatism, empiricism, and other outdated ideas and successfully carry out their work as required by the Party and thus to develop our economy at a faster pace and more satisfactorily."

Who, then, were these cadres and why did they retain these antiquated ideas? The problem evidently has to do with the "old cadres." According to the president, "the old cadres who are now working in various domains of the national economy are all valuable treasures of our Party." These cadres "have done a great deal of work and played an important role in the past." But, in spite of continued exhortations to study and keep up with modern ideas, these cadres evidently failed to keep abreast of the rapidly changing situation:

> With the lapse of three decades following liberation, however, they have now reached an old age and their level, too, fails to keep pace with the rapidly developing realities. Our Party established a system of collective study such as the Saturday study and Wednesday lecture, and a system in which they devote themselves solely to study at regular schools a month every year, so that they may not lag behind the developing realities. But they cannot successfully press forward with socialist construction nor can they wage energetically the speedy battle required by the Party only with the knowledge and experience they have now, [when] the economy has largely grown in scale and modern science and technology are required in all domains of economic construction.

What should be done with these old cadres? The choice was clearly between discarding them or re-educating them. Since they had been continually subjected to the process of re-education, the choice was actually between discarding them or providing them with intensive guidance, not only in the realm of technology but in the realm of ideology and culture. By lagging behind modern science and technology, these old cadres failed not only in the task of bringing about technical revolution but also, by implication, in other aspects as well. Hence they were to be subjected to the guidance of the Three-Revolution Teams. The leader said: "And yet, we should not divorce all the old cadres from work or dismiss them. We must value them. We must not dismiss the old cadres but lend them a good help so that they may do work well and continue to keep the flowers in bloom in the future too, as they did in the past. It was for this purpose that our Party formed the Three-Revolution Teams. . . ."

The tasks assigned to the Three-Revolution Teams were specific enough. According to the president:

> We told the members of the Three-Revolution Teams: You comrades should go down to teach and help the cadres. The target of struggle you should aim at is conservatism, empiricism, bureaucratism, and other outdated ideas in the minds of the cadres, not the cadres themselves. Therefore, you must wage an uncompromising struggle against the outdated ideas in their minds, but you must respect and help them. We also told the members of the Three-Revolution Teams that they should go down to teach to cadres modern sciences and techniques and show them the might of modern sciences and techniques through practice as the cadres are low in level and fail to study regularly, busying themselves only with the practical work.

Conservatism and bureaucratism are obvious enough "errors" that need to be rectified, and the North Korean leader had criticized these tendencies among the cadres on numerous occasions before. But what is the "empiricism" that the old cadres are criticized for? An authoritative North Korean source, the *Dictionary of Philosophy,* provides the following definition:[32]

> The thought and behavior pattern that ignores the developing realities, scientific researches, and creative attitude and persists in the old experiences. Empiricism exaggerates the significance of old experiences, tries to fit the knowledge gained from experiences into the newly developed realities through stale formulas.[33] It prevents the correct awareness of realities by slighting the new theories and thus hinders our progress.

The dictionary further states that empiricists hang on to the "announced capacity" (as in a machine), and do not trust the creativity of the masses and the might of the reform movement of the masses. All in all, empiricism is equated with passivity and conservatism. In order to overcome empiricism, one is required thoroughly to arm oneself with the party's policy line, and acquire the "revolutionary method" of deeply studying the incessantly progressing realities and thoroughly relying on the masses. Thus, the struggle against empiricism is regarded as an integral part of implementing the party's mass line.

Seen in the context of the party's effort to push forward technological advancement and ideological revolution, empiricism is thus one of the cardinal errors to be rectified. It is also quite obvious that the "old cadres," whose status in the party depends mostly on experience rather than on the level of educational attainment, would be prone to commit that error. Equally obvious is the fact that for most of the old cadres, empiricism would have been the most difficult tendency to be surmounted.

Given the purpose of the Three-Revolution Teams, one can easily anticipate the characteristics of the members of these teams. According to the president, these teams consisted of functionaries of the Party Central Committee and other party workers, functionaries of the state and economic organs, functionaries of the working people's organizations (such as the labor union), scientific and technical personnel, and young intellectuals. Since the main purpose was to re-educate the old cadres, it was natural that the Three-Revolution Teams consisted mostly of the younger cadres. According to the leader, "tens of thousands of young intellectuals" have been "embraced" in these teams. Included in these teams were many scientists and young intellectuals "possessed of the knowledge of modern sciences."

The size of these teams varied according to the size of the factories and enterprises targeted. For the "ordinary" factories and enterprises, a team consisting of twenty to thirty members was assigned. For "big" factories and enterprises, some fifty persons were assigned. They were dispatched to each workshop and each work team to "see how things go there and to guide them at the production sites." They were to grasp clearly the essence of the defects manifested at work and give substantial help to the guiding personnel and workers of the factories and enterprises so they might "make a good job of their work, displaying creative ingenuity." According to the leader, this was "a work method incomparably superior to the work method of the past, when one or two instructors were sent down to dig up defects."

The leader announced in March 1975 that the Three-Revolution Teams attained great successes "above all in the fulfillment of the ideological revolution." But given the serious nature of the problems indicated, an outsider could not help but to wonder whether the campaign could eradicate all the problems, particularly in turning the old cadres around. The old cadres, of course, would have retreated in the face of this onslaught from the central headquarters. But, unless they can somehow prove the value of their experience, their days are numbered. Even if they eagerly wish to change, many of the old cadres may find it simply impossible to follow the command. The subtle struggle, therefore, is likely to continue, and it may lead eventually to a more dramatic and massive purge.

Not only has the importance of technically trained personnel been emphasized in North Korea, but their numbers have significantly increased during the past decade and a half. President Kim Il-sŏng announced at the Fifth Congress that there were 497,000 engineers, assistant engineers, and specialists, and that this was 4.3 times the number in 1960.[34] This would mean that there were only 115,581 of them in 1960. By 1976 the number had reached one million, a nine-fold increase.[35] Approximately 40 percent of this one million are presumably college graduates.[36] In the meantime, as we related earlier, the number of KWP members had increased from 1,311,563 in 1961 to approximately two million in 1975. Given the party's emphasis on cultural and technical revolutions during the same period, one could hypothesize that a larger percentage of technical personnel have been admitted to the KWP. It is also relevant to indicate that over 60 percent of the North Korean work force engages in non-agrarian work.[37] Given all this, one can easily understand the rapid rise of the technocrats in the KWP membership. The old cadres, therefore, would still be under increasing pressure even if the top leadership had not dispatched the Three-Revolution Teams.

It is indeed possible that the dispatch of the Three-Revolution Teams was a signal that North Korea has entered a new era. In the old era the party had served as a unique route to power and prestige. Being admitted to the party meant being elevated to an elite status, with proximity to the source of all power. "Purity" in family background, ideological commitment, and loyalty to the supreme leader had outweighed all other considerations in being admitted to elite status. But by dispatching young scientists and intellectuals to "re-educate" the old cadres who were allegedly saddled with outmoded ideas, the leader acknowledged a change in the priority of values. Of course, ideological commitment and loyalty to the leader are still the essential requirements for membership in the North Korean elite. But these qualifications are of common currency in the North Korean society today, rather than being the exclusive property of party members. It is therefore natural for the supreme leader to place more value on the newly educated scientists and specialists than on the old cadres, whose education and training are now inadequate. The "political entrepreneurs" without special functional expertise must accommodate themselves to the emergence of the new technocrats.

Indeed, some of the provisions in the new constitution of the DPRK adopted in December 1972 reflect the broad range of homogeneity attained in North Korea and suggest the possibility that the distinction between party members and others may be muted in the future. Article 3 of the constitution declares, for example, that the DPRK is a "revolutionary state power." Article 7 says that the "sovereignty of the DPRK rests with the workers, peasants, soldiers, and working intellectuals." Article 68 states, on the other hand that "Citizens must display a high degree of collectivist spirit. Citizens must cherish their collective and organization and establish the revolutionary trait of working devotedly for the sake of society and the people and for the sake of the homeland and the revolution."[38] Thus even ordinary citizens are the constituents of a "revolutionary state power" with duties to work for the revolution. While members of the KWP are supposedly the "vanguard" of the working class and "all the toiling masses" of the society, those members of the vanguard who fail to perform adequately could not be accorded better status than the non-KWP members who contribute significantly to the technical revolution.

Just as communists everywhere, the KWP takes its membership very seriously, and it is not likely that the party will co-opt all the scientists and specialists. But since applicants to institutions of higher learning are strictly screened by the party to assure purity in background and since every inhabitant of North Korea has been subjected to rigorous ideological indoctrination, the party would have every reason to equalize opportunity among party members and non-party technocrats. Of course, the leader had long spoken of the "core members" as a special category of membership, and those members will remain as the true elite in the communist society. But others in the party who have not successfully mastered the norms of technical revolution may find their status outstripped by the young intellectuals.

CONCLUSIONS

The two decades since the purge of the last remnant of the Yenan faction in 1958 have been truly the Kim Il-sŏng era in North Korea. During this period, the Korean Workers' Party has been turned into an intensely personal party in which everything revolves around its supreme leader. A body of hagiology has been created around the leader and his family to command the present and to define the future. Every word he uttered and is presumed to have uttered during the last half century has been incorporated into the hagiology to serve as a directive for the party. True to form, these canonical writings have been supplemented by a large number of testimonials by disciples of varying proximity to the leader, with the sole intent of confirming the supremacy of the national-savior incarnate.

The vocabulary of the KWP is Marxist-Leninist and its rituals are secular and modern, but one could draw a close parallel between the form and content of the KWP and those of many religious bodies. All evidence leads to the conclusion that the members of the KWP have unabashed and unswerving faith in the leader, and that this faith is refreshed daily by canonical readings. No other communist party in the world appears to have cultivated as strong a faith in its leadership. Unlike the CCP or the CPSU, the KWP does not permit self-doubt, self-ridicule, cynicism, or mild dissension even in a humorous vein. President Kim's words must be followed relentlessly in dead seriousness.

If President Kim's words constitute the soul of the KWP, the party's organizational mechanisms serve as its body; and this body has been forged according to the will of the leader to obey every whim and command from the center. The two million members linked together in the organization find their identity, and indeed their purpose in life, only by striving to fulfill the leader's directives. To think otherwise is to invite trouble. Any temptation to indulge in private thoughts that are not in line with the commands of the leader must be quickly suppressed, lest such thought have an effect upon one's behavior and actions.

The fact that there is a high rate of turnover in the upper reaches of the party elite, as well as the fact that the party found it necessary to conduct the Three Revolutions Campaign between 1974 and 1975 do indicate, however, that the KWP has not yet attained the conditions it desires. Among those who failed the test were many of those who had maintained close bonds with the supreme leader since the 1930s. Loyalty alone is no longer enough. The system demands performance.

As we have seen, the criteria of performance is also beginning to affect the careers of some of the trusted cadres at lower levels. In spite of constant exhortations, the party inevitably produced stragglers. The generation that had pulled the party through the most difficult period since the war seems to be lagging behind and impeding the party's advance into the new era. For the time being, the leadership appears to have decided to give the older generation another chance to redeem itself. But one cannot be very sanguine about their future.

North Korea has undergone great transformations since 1958, when the party declared that the northern half of the country was entering into the socialist era. Virtually nothing in the society remains unchanged. Revolution in ideology, culture, and technology—the goals pursued by the party—could not fail to touch the life of every inhabitant. As we suggested earlier, these changes have begun to affect the Korean Workers' Party itself. In the long run, the infusion of a large number of technocrats into the party canot fail to affect the character of the party, although under normal circumstances it would take decades for the new generation to significantly affect the course of the party. But the forces of change have only begun to affect the party. One cannot accurately predict where they may lead once they acquire momentum.

Notes

1. THE ORIGINS

1. For the latest and most detailed official biography of Kim Il-sŏng, see Baik Bong, *Kim Il Sung: Biography*, 3 vols. (Tokyo, 1969–1970).

2. For example, see Center for Historical Studies, Academy of Science, DPRK, *Chosŏn t'ongsa* (An Outline History of Korea), Pyongyang, 1958, II, 219–304.

3. The best biography available is by Yu Sŏk-in, *Aeguk ui pyŏl dŭl* (The Patriotic Stars), Seoul, 1965, pp. 176–208.

4. Manchukuo, Gunseibu, Komonbu (Military Department, Advisory Section), *Manshū kyōsanhi no kenkyū* (A Study of Communist Insurgents in Manchuria), n.p., 1937, p. 543.

5. Hayashi Raisaburō, *Senjin dokuritsu undō ni kansuru chōsa hōkohusho* (Report on the Korean Independence Movement), Tokyo, 1920, pp. 17–18.

6. Japanese Ministry of Foreign Affairs, "Kōrai Kyōsanto oyobi Zenro Kyōsanto no gaikyō" (An Outline of the Koryo Communist Party and the All-Russian Communist Party), November 1922, in Archives of the Japanese Ministry of Foreign Affairs, 1867–1945, microfilmed for the Library of Congress, Reel S 721 (S. 9.4.5.2–30), frame 44180 (hereinafter cited as AJMFA).

7. V. Lenin, *Collected Works*, XIX, 55, from *Vorbote*, No. 2, April 1916. Italics in original. Quoted from Allan Whiting, *Soviet Policies in China, 1917–1924* (New York, 1953), p. 16.

8. Ibid., p. 22.

9. Han Hyŏng-gwŏn, "Hyŏngmyŏng-ga ui hoesangrok" (Recollections of a Revolutionary), *Samch'ŏlli* (Three Thousand Ri), Seoul, October 1, 1948, p. 10.

10. For details, see "The Origins of the Korean Communist Movement (I)," *Journal of Asian Studies*, XX (1), November 1960, p. 17.

11. Archives of the Japanese Army, Navy, and Other Agencies, 1876–1945, microfilmed for the Library of Congress, Reel 122, frames 36729–30 (hereinafter cited as AJAN).

12. "Kōrai Kyōsanto oyobi Zenro Kyōsantō," op. cit.

13. Hu Ch'aio-mu, *Chungkuo kungch'antang ti sanshih-nien* (Thirty Years of the Chinese Communist Party), Peking, 1952, p. 15.

14. "Kōrai Kyōsanto oyobi Zenro Kyōsantō," op. cit.

15. Chōsen Sōtokufu, Hōmu-kyoku (Bureau of Justice, Korean Government-General), *Chōsen dokuritsu shisō undō no hensen* (Changes in the Korean Independence Thought Movement), Seoul, 1931, p. 44.

16. Xenia Joukoff Eudin and Robert C. North, *Soviet Russia and the East, 1920–1927, A Documentary Survey* (Stanford, California, 1957), p. 462.

17. Kōrai Kyōsanto oyobi Zenro Kyōsantō, op. cit.

2. INTELLIGENTSIA AND COMMUNISM IN KOREA

1. Kim Yak-su's background is taken from his "Killim kwa Namkyŏng e-sŏ" (In Chilin and Nanking), *Samch'ŏlli*, January 1932, pp. 33–34. For a most detailed and definitive account of the activities of the Korean students in Japan in this period, see Kim Jun-yŏp and Kim Ch'ang-sun, *Hanguk Kongsan chui undong-sa* (History of the Korean Communist Movement), Seoul, 1969–1975, II, 29–41 (hereinafter cited as Kim and Kim).

2. For details, see "Preliminary Trial Statement of Kim Ch'an," in Kōtō Hōin, Kenjikyoku (Prosecutor's Office, High Court, Korean Government-General), *Shisō geppō* (Thought Monthly), Vol. 2, No. 2, May 1932, no pagination. A copy of this report is in AJMFA, Reels S356–357, photographic frames 1880–1903.

3. *Tong-a Ilbo* (East Asia Daily, Seoul), August 5, 1923, and Kim and Kim, II, 38.

4. The number of Korean students in Japan at the secondary level or above was as follows (as of December of each year): 592 in 1918, 448 in 1919, 980 in 1920, 1,516 in 1921, and 1,912 in 1922. See Yoshiura Daizō, *Chōsenjin no kyōsan shungi undō* (Communist Movements of the Koreans), Bureau of Criminal Affairs, Ministry of Justice, Thought Study Material Series (Shisō kenkyū shiryō), number 71, (Tokyo, 1940), p. 13.

5. Kim Sŏng-suk interview, Seoul, September 11, 1966. Mr. Kim worked closely with the early leaders of the communist movement. According to Mr. Kim, it was Hong Saeng-gyu who brought Kim Tu-jŏn, Yi Myŏng-gŏn, and Kim Won-bong together and made them blood brothers in the fight for Korean independence, naming them respectively Yak-su (like water), Yŏ-sŏng (like a star), and Yak-san (like a mountain). Kim Yak-su and Yi Yŏ-sŏng were together in the North Star Society in Tokyo. Kim Yak-san was with Kim Yak-su when he

was in Antung, Manchuria (now Tantung), but unlike Yak-su, he decided to remain in China. He subsequently became a leader of the terrorist group known as Ui-yŏl-tan, which came to be feared by the Japanese. Yi Yŏ-sŏng's funds were also liberally used for Kim Yak-san's operations.

6. Chŏng T'ae-sin was a leading member of the Friends' Society of the Working Students in Tokyo and a close friend of Kim Yak-su.

7. Yi Pong-su was a Meiji University graduate. Chu Chong-gŏn was a graduate of an agricultural college in Tokyo. Kim Ch'ŏl-su was a graduate of Waseda University. Thus, many of these individuals were influenced by the ideological currents in Tokyo.

8. For details, see Kim and Kim, II, 33.

9. Ibid., p. 36.

10. Ibid., p. 36, citing *Tong-a Ilbo*, December 24, 1922.

11. The number of wage earners between 1920 and 1923 is estimated to be as follows: factory workers, 55,000; miners, 18,000; stevedores, 10,000. For details, see Kim Yun-hwan, *Il-che-ha Hanguk nodong undong ui chŏn-gae kwajŏng* (The Developmental Process of the Labor Movement in Korea under Japanese Imperialism), Ph.D. dissertation, Korea University, 1968, chapters II and III.

12. The Communist International, *From the Fourth to the Fifth World Congress, Report of the Executive Committee of the Communist International* (London, 1924), p. 76.

13. Resolution of 1925, quoted in Otto Kuusinen, "O koreiskom kommunistcheskom dvizhenii" (On the Korean Communist Movement), *Revolyutsionnyi vostok*, Moscow, Nos. 11–12, 1931, pp. 99–116. For an English translation, see Dae-Sook Suh (ed.), *Documents of Korean Communism, 1918–1948* (Princeton, 1970), pp. 257–282.

14. Ibid.

15. Kim Yun-hwan, III, 46–49. (Roman numeral indicates chapter number).

16. Ibid., II, 30.

17. Ibid., II, 30.

18. Ibid., II, 32.

19. For details, see ibid., III, 46–60, and Kim and Kim, II, 92–101.

20. For details, see Keijō Chihō Hōin, Kenji-Kyoku, Shisō-bu (Thought Section, Prosecutor's Office, Seoul District Court), *Chōsen Kyōsantō jiken* (The Korean Communist Party Incident), Seoul, n.d., pp. 5–6.

21. *Hesŏng* (Comet, Seoul), September 1931, p. 54.

22. Kim and Kim, II, 367.

23. Ibid., II, 365–447 provides the details. Also see *Chōsen Kyōsantō jiken.*

24. Robert A. Scalapino, *The Japanese Communist Movement, 1920–1966* (Berkeley, California, 1967), pp. 21–22.

25. For the full theses of the Executive Committee of the Communist International, see *International Press Correspondence*, Vol. 9, No. 8 (February 15, 1929), pp. 130–133, or Suh, *Documents*, pp. 243–256.

26. *International Press Correspondence*, Vol. 9, No. 8, p. 131.

3. SOCIAL BASIS OF AN AGRARIAN REVOLUTION

1. From the December Theses. In Suh, *Documents*, pp. 244–246.

2. Kim Yong-gi, *Chosŏn ui nongŏp* (Agriculture in Korea), Seoul, 1946, p. 12.

3. Zenkoku Keizai Chōsa Kikan Rengōkai Chōsen Shibu (Federation of Economic Study Agencies throughout Japan, Korean Branch) (ed.), *Chōsen Keizai Nempō* (Korean Economy Annual Report), 1941–1942 ed. (Tokyo, 1943), p. 233.

4. Ibid., p. 229.

5. Ibid., p. 229.

6. Chōsen Nōkai (Agricultural Association of Korea), *Chōsen nōgyō hattatsu-shi, Seisaku-hen* (History of the Agricultural Development in Korea, Policy Part), Seoul, 1944, pp. 526–527.

7. Andrew J. Grajdanzev, *Modern Korea* (New York, 1944), p. 113.

8. *Chōsen nōgyō hattatsu-shi*, p. 543.

9. Grajdanzev, *Modern Korea*, p. 114.

10. Shihō-shō, Keiji-kyoku (Bureau of Criminal Affairs, Ministry of Justice, Japan), *Chōsenjin no kyōsan shugi undō* (Communist Movements of the Koreans), Shisō Kenkyū Shiryō (Thought Study Material), No. 71 (Tokyo, 1939), p. 1.

11. Kung-chuan Hsiao, *Rural China: Imperial Control in the Nineteenth Century* (Seattle, 1960), p. 511.

12. Ibid., p. 511.

13. Chōsen Nōkai, *Chōsen nōgyō hattatsu-shi*, p. 535.

14. Ibid., p. 536.

15. Ibid., pp. 536–538.

16. "Tasks of the Revolutionary Trade Union Movement in Korea," resolution adopted by the R. I. L. U. (Red International of Labour Unions or Profintern) Executive Bureau of September 18, 1930, reprinted in English in Red International of Labour Unions, *Resolutions* (London, 1931), pp. 152–158.

17. Based on various reports and court trial documents in Kōtō Hōin, Kenjikyoku (Prosecutor's Bureau, High Court, Korean Government-General) *Shisō ihō*, No. 3, pp. 27–47; ibid., No. 4, pp. 32–54; *Shisō geppō* (Thought Monthly, the predecessor of *Shisō ihō*), Vol. 4, No. 4, pp. 16–21, and Vol. 3, No. 6, p. 5.

18. The details are available in *Shisō geppō*, Vol. 3, No. 12 (March 1934), pp. 13–44.

19. Ibid., Vol. 3, No. 1 (April 1933), pp. 29–40.

20. The details of this movement are provided in *Shisō ihō*, No. 8, pp. 12–23, and No. 11, pp. 147–151.

21. Ibid., No. 14, pp. 48–49.

22. Ibid., No. 11 (June 1937), pp. 147–148.

23. Ibid., No. 11, pp. 146–170.

24. *Manshū kyōsanhi no kenkyū*, pp. 503–505.

25. *Chōsen nōgnō hattatsu-shi*, pp. 540–542.

26. Ibid., p. 543.

27. Chōsen Sōtokufu, Keimukyoku (Police Affairs Bureau, Korean Government-General), *Saikin ni okeru Chōsen chian jōkyō* (Recent Conditions of Public Security in Korea), Seoul, 1934, pp. 156–158. Between 1920 and 1933 inclusive, there were 13 cases of tenant disputes with 1,741 persons involved in South Hamgyŏng Province, but only one case with 14 persons in North Hamgyŏng Province. This can be contrasted with South Chŏlla Province, which had 122 cases involving 9,722 persons; South Kyŏngsang Province, with 215 cases involving 7,963 persons; and Hwanghae Province, with 91 cases involving 8,105 persons.

28. Minsei-bu, Sōmu-shi, Chōsaka (Research Section, General Affairs Division, Department of Civil Administration, Manchukuo), *Zaiman Chōsenjin jijō* (Condition of the Koreans in Manchuria), Changchun, 1933, pp. 19–22.

29. *Saikin ni okeru Chōsen no chian jōkyō*, 1934, p. 48.

30. *Shisō ihō*, No. 11, pp. 146–170.

31. For details, see *Manshū kyōsanhi no kenkyū*, pp. 79–87.

32. From the December Theses, in Suh, *Documents*, p. 247.

33. Ibid., p. 248.

34. See note 16 above for reference to the September theses.

35. The details are available in Robert A. Scalapino and Chong-Sik Lee, *Communism in Korea* (Berkeley, California, 1973), pp. 112–119.

4. ANTI-JAPANESE STRUGGLES AND THE KOREAN COMMUNISTS IN CHINA

1. "The Establishment of the Korean National Liberation United Front centering around Wonsan, South Hamgyŏng Province, and the Disturbance of the Rear Area," *Shisō ihō*, No. 21, pp. 179–192.

2. *Saikin ni okeru Chōsen chian jōkyō*, 1934, p. 290.

3. See John J. Stephan, "The Korean Minority in the Soviet Union," *Mizan*, December 1971, pp. 138–150, and Chong-Sik Lee and Ki-wan Oh, "The Russian Faction in North Korea," *Asian Survey*, April 1968, pp. 270–288.

4. For details, see Chong-Sik Lee, *The Politics of Korean Nationalism* (Berkeley, 1963), Chapters 8–12.

5. See Scalapino and Lee, *Communism in Korea*, Vol. 1, pp. 142–157.

6. Ibid., pp. 170–180; Dae-Sook Suh, *The Korean Communist Movement, 1918–1948* (Princeton, 1968), pp. 202–230.

7. A news item in *Jen-min Jih-pao* (People's Daily, Peking), July 11, 1964, reporting on the construction of the Chinese-Korean Friendship Monument in

Canton, referred to "150 Korean comrades of the Whampoa Military Academy, most of whom have been sacrificed during the course of the struggle." Kim San and Nym Wales, *Song of Ariran: A Life Story of a Korean Rebel* (New York, 1941, reprinted, San Francisco, n.d.), p. 160, refers to an estimated 200 Koreans participating in the Canton Commune uprising. Kim San allegedly participated in the uprising.

8. In view of the fact that the surname "Mu" (pronounced "Wu" in Chinese) is not known among Korean genealogists, it is probably safe to assume that Mu Chŏng is an adopted name.

9. Naimu-shō, Keiho-kyoku (Police and Security Bureau, Ministry of Home Affairs, Japan), *Tokkō geppō* (Special Higher Police Monthly Report), April 1941, pp. 97–101.

10. *Chieh-fang Jih-pao* (Yenan), February 13, 1944.

11. On September 21, 1942, a memorial service was held for eleven Koreans who had been killed in action. Chu Teh, the commander-in-chief of the Chinese communist forces, made a brief speech. In the course of his speech, he said, "Do you know Li Hung-kwang (Yi Hong-gwang in Korean)? He was a Korean, but he joined the Northeastern Volunteer Army and worked actively in it." Ibid., September 21, 1942. Yi Hong-gwang was one of the early leaders of the guerrilla movement in the Manchurian hinterland whose struggles eventually led to the establishment of the Northeastern Anti-Japanese Allied Army.

12. A more detailed study of the communist movement in Manchuria is being prepared by the author; the outline presented here is excerpted from this study.

13. The number of anti-Japanese fighters killed, by Japanese account, was 7,591 in 1932, 8,728 in 1933, and 8,909 in 1934. Manshūkoku-shi Hensan Kankōkai (Society to Compile and Publish the History of Manchukuo), *Manshūkoku-shi* (History of Manchukuo), Tokyo, 1971, II, 312.

14. Ibid., II, 303.

15. The Central Committee of the CCP, however, contradicted the instructions from the Comintern, which had been sent in the form a letter from Wang Ming, the CCP's representative in Moscow. Details of this dispute will be set forth in my forthcoming work on the Communist movement in Manchuria.

16. Based on Feng Chung-yün, *Tung-pei K'angjih Lien-chün shih-ssu-nien k'u-tou chien-shih* (Brief History of the Fourteen Years of the Northeastern Anti-Japanese Allied Army), Harbin, 1946; Chi Yun-lung, *Yang Ching-yü ho K'ang Lien Ti-i-lu Chün* (Yang Ching-Yu and the First Route Army of the Anti-Japanese Allied Army), n.p., 1946; Sun Chieh, *Tungpei K'ang-Jih Lien-chün ti-ssu-chün* (The Fourth Army of the Northeastern Anti-Japanese Allied Army), Paris(?), 1936; and *Manshūkoku-shi, Manshū kyōsanhi no kenkyū,* and other articles.

17. Feng Chung-yün, pp. 34–39.

18. *Manshūkoku-shi*, p. 320.

19. Ibid., pp. 320–321.

20. Ibid., pp. 321–325.

21. Ibid., p. 325.

22. *Chieh-fang jih-pao* (Yenan), September 21, 1942 (see note 11 above).

23. Chi Yun-lung (note 16 above), pp. 106–107.

24. *Manshū kyōsanhi no kenkyū*, pp. 339–342.

25. See my "Witch Hunt Among the Guerrillas: The Min-Sheng-T'uan Incident," *China Quarterly*, April–June 1966, pp. 107–117.

26. *Manshū kyōsanhi no kenkyū*, p. 394.

27. *Shisō ihō*, No. 25 (December 1940), p. 66. Evidently Wei had kept copies of letters he had sent, and these were captured by Japanese troops during a raid. Wei apparently was unaware that Wang Ming and K'ang Sheng had gone to Yenan in 1938.

28. Feng Chung-yün, pp. 31, 36–41.

29. *Manshūkoku-shi*, p. 325.

30. Scalapino and Lee, *Communism in Korea*, pp. 226–270, presents our previous analysis.

31. Wei Cheng-min's documents indicate that he had sent or was about to send a number of the old and wounded veterans, as well as some of the wavering elements in the rank-and-file, to the Soviet Union in 1940. See *Shisō ihō*, No. 25, pp. 77, 80.

5. THE BEGINNING OF THE NEW ERA IN NORTH KOREA

1. Milovan Djilas, *Conversations with Stalin* (New York, 1962), p. 114.

2. The facts discussed above are treated in detail in Scalapino and Lee, *Communism in Korea*, pp. 327–331.

3. The minutes of this conference are in Chosŏn Sanŏp Nodong Chosaso (Research Center for Korean Industry and Labor), (eds.), *Ol-ŭn nosŏn* (The Correct Line), Seoul, 1945 (reprinted by Minjung Shinmunsa, Tokyo, 1946), pp. 30–48. English translation is available in Chong-Sik Lee (ed.), *Materials on Korean Communism, 1945–1947* (Honolulu, 1977), pp. 231–244. The establishment of the North Korean Bureau was proposed by Kim Il-sŏng.

4. For the best account of the events of these days, see Morita Yoshio, *Chōsen shūsen no kiroku* (The Record of the End of the War in Korea), Tokyo, 1964, pp. 76–85.

5. Scalapino and Lee, *Communism in Korea*, pp. 315–317.

6. These documents are available in the following two publications issued by the Asiatic Research Center of Korea University, Seoul: Kim Jun-yŏp, *et al.* (eds.), *Puk Han yŏngu charyojip* (Materials on North Korean Studies), I (Seoul, 1968); and Ch'a Rak-hun and Chŏng Kyŏng-mo (eds.), *Pak-Han pŏpryŏng yŏnhyŏkjip* (North Korean Laws), I (Seoul, 1969).

7. For this speech, which among other things spelled out North Korea's unification strategy, see *Kim Il-sŏng sŏnjip* (Selected Works of Kim Il-sŏng), Pyongyang, 1963 edition, I, 15–28.

8. Han Im-hyŏk, *Kim Il-sŏng tongji e ŭihan Chosŏn Kongsandang ch'ang-gŏn* (The Founding of the Korean Communist Party by Comrade Kim Il-sŏng), Pyongyang, 1961, p. 55.

9. Scalapino and Lee, *Communism in Korea*, p. 322.

10. Ibid., pp. 338–340.

11. In December 1945 there were only 4,530 KCP members in North Korea. By July–August 1946, this number had expanded to 276,000 members. The New People's Party, on the other hand, reportedly had only 90,000 members as of August 1946. See ibid., p. 172.

12. It should be noted that no systematic study has ever been made of the New People's Party. The information presented here, based on some Korean accounts, must be regarded as tentative.

13. Kim Il-sŏng, "All for the Preparation of Our Democratic Strength," in *Kŭlloja* (The Workers, the organ of the NKWP), No. 1, October 1946, pp. 7–8; and Kim Il-sŏng, "Conclusions on Questions and Discussion," ibid., pp. 30–34. Even though Kim Il-sŏng was elected vice-chairman of the Central Executive Committee, his speech was printed ahead of the one given by Kim Tu-bong, who was elected chairman.

14. Ibid., p. 30.

15. For details, see Scalapino and Lee, *Communism in Korea*, p. 712.

16. For details, see ibid., pp. 368–372.

17. Nikita Khrushchev, *Khrushchev Remembers* (Boston, 1970), pp. 367–373.

18. The Research Institute of History, Academy of Sciences of the Democratic People's Republic of Korea, *History of the Just Fatherland Liberation War of the Korean People* (Pyongyang, 1961), p. 28. Quoted from the English text.

19. Ibid., p. 29.

20. "Every Effort for Victory in the War," radio address to the entire Korean people, June 26, 1950, in Kim Il-sŏng, *Selected Works*, I (Pyongyang, 1971), p.294.

21. Ibid., p. 294.

22. For an excellent analysis of the decision-making process in Washington after the North Korean invasion, see Glenn D. Paige, *The Korean Decision, June 24–30, 1950* (New York, 1968).

23. For a detailed account of the early battles of the war, see Roy E. Appleman, *South to the Naktong, North to the Yalu (June–November 1950)* (Washington, 1961).

24. M. S. Kapitsa, *KNR: dva desyatiletiya—dve politiki* (The People's Republic of China: Two Decades, Two Policies), Moscow, 1969, pp. 36–37; and O. B. Borisov and B. T. Koloskov, *Sovetsko-Kitaiski Otnosheniya 1945–1970, kratikii ocherk* (Soviet-Chinese Relations, 1945–1970, A Brief Essay), Moscow, 1971, pp. 55ff.

25. The Three Year Plan, *Kyŏngje kŏnsŏl* (Economic Construction), September 1956, pp. 5–6.

26. *Kim Il-sŏng sŏnjip* (Selected Works of Kim Il-sŏng), 1960 edition, IV, 385.

6. TOWARD A PARTY OF KIM IL-SŎNG

1. Kim's report to the Third Plenum, delivered December 21, 1950, entitled "Present Conditions and Tasks at Hand," is contained in *Kin Nichisei senshū* (Selected Works of Kim Il-sŏng), Japanese ed., Kyoto, 1952, II, 105–144. While earlier editions of Kim's collected works, such as *Chayu wa tongnip ŭl wihan Chosŏn inmin ŭi chŏngui ui choguk haebang chŏnjaeng* (The Korean People's Just Fatherland Liberation War for Freedom and Independence, Pyongyang, 1954), included this report, more recent editions conspicuously omit it. See, for example, Kim Il Sung, *Selected Works*, Pyongyang, 1971, Vol. 1, and *Kim Il-sŏng chŏjak sŏnjip* (Selected Writings of Kim Il-sŏng), Pyongyang, 1967, Vol. 1.

2. Kim's report to the Fourth Plenum, delivered on November 1, 1951, entitled "On Some Defects in the Organizational Work of Party Organizations," is in *Selected Works* (English edition, 1971), I, 313–336.

3. Kim's report to the Fifth Plenum, delivered on December 15, 1952, entitled "The Organizational and Ideological Consolidation of the Party is the Basis of Our Victory," is in *Selected Works*, I, 371–412.

4. "For the Establishment of a United Party of the Working Masses," in *Selected Works*, I, 74–89 (at pp. 83–85).

5. Kim's report is in *Selected Works*, I, 204–257. His discussion of the shortcomings of the party is on pp. 244–247.

6. Ibid., I, 317.

7. Ibid., I, 320.

8. Ibid., I, 321.

9. Ibid., I, 388.

10. Ibid., I, 390.

11. *Kim Il-sŏng sŏnjip*, IV, 344.

12. Ibid., IV, 267.

13. Chong-Sik Lee and Ki-Wan Oh, "The Russian Faction in North Korea," *Asian Survey*, April 1968, 270–288 (at pp. 275–276).

14. *Selected Works*, I, 396–397.

15. Scalapino and Lee, *Communism in Korea*, p. 439.

16. Ibid., pp. 440–447.

17. Ibid., pp. 447–451.

18. "Army-Party Relations in the Light of the Cultural Revolution," in John Wilson Lewis (ed.), *Party Leadership and Revolutionary Power in China* (New York, 1970), p. 379.

19. For details of the Three-Year Plan, see *Communism in Korea*, pp. 527–535, 1211–1217; Kim Il-sŏng, "Everything for the Postwar Rehabilitation and Development of the National Economy," report delivered at the Sixth Plenary Meeting of the Central Committee, August 5, 1953, in *Selected Works*, I, 413–462.

20. Ibid., I, 501–517.

21. Ibid., I, 504.

22. Ibid., I, 506.

23. See, for example, Mao's "On Methods of Leadership," (1943), in *Selected Works of Mao Tse-tung* (New York, 1954–56), IV, 111–117. For a discussion of the Chinese style of leadership, see John Wilson Lewis, *Leadership in Communist China* (Ithica, New York, 1963), chapter III.

24. Kim Il Sung, *Selected Works*, I, 533.

25. Ibid., I, 536–537.

26. Ibid., I, 538.

27. Ibid., I, 540–554. The North Korean translators used the English word "bureaucracy" for "Kwanryo chuui" in the 1971 edition of the *Selected Works*, but the more accurate translation would be "bureaucratism." I have replaced the word "bureaucracy" with "bureaucratism" even when quoting directly from the English edition of the above work here.

28. Ibid., I, 541.

29. Ibid., I, 542.

30. Ibid., I, 547.

31. Ibid., I, 544.

32. Ibid., I, 573.

33. Ibid., I, 582–606. The North Koreans spell *chuch'e*, which is in accordance with the McCune-Reischauer system, as *Juche*.

34. For the background and career of Pak and other Russian-Koreans, see Lee and Oh, "Russian Faction," pp. 270–288.

35. Kim Il-Sung, *Selected Works*, I, 584.

36. Ibid., I, 586–587.

37. Ibid., I, 592.

38. Ibid., I, 589.

39. *Kim Il-sŏng sŏnjip*, 1960 ed., IV, 346. This paragraph was omitted from *Kim Il-sŏng chŏjak sŏnjip* (Selected Writings of Kim Il-sŏng), 1967, I, 578, and *Selected Works* (English edition, 1971), I, 600.

40. I had argued earlier that among other things, the Russian reluctance to intervene in the Korean War in the darkest hours for the North Korean forces probably contributed toward Kim Il-sŏng's turn toward nationalism. See "Stalinism in the East: Communism in North Korea," in Robert A. Scalapino (ed.), *The Communist Revolution in Asia* (Englewood Cliffs, N.J., 1965), pp. 135–136.

41. *Selected Works*, I, 602.

42. Ibid., I, 601–602.

43. Pak Yŏn-baek, "The Historical Significance of the Second Party Congress," *Kŭlloja*, February 1957, pp. 23–34. Quoted from Scalapino and Lee, *Communism in Korea*, p. 521.

44. "The Leninist Unity of the CPSU Is Invulnerable," *Kŭlloja*, July 1957.

45. Kim Il-sŏng, "The Friendship and Solidarity of Socialist Countries," *Kŭlloja*, November 1957, pp. 8–15.

46. Kim Ch'ang-sun, *Puk-Han sip-o-nyŏn sa* (Fifteen-Year History of North Korea), Seoul, 1961, pp. 156–157.

47. "For the Successful Fulfillment of the First Five-Year Plan," Concluding Speech at the First Conference of the Workers' Party of Korea, March 6, 1958, in *Selected Works*, II, 102–131 (at p. 124).

48. Ibid., p. 125.

49. Ibid., p. 128.

50. Ibid., p. 129.

7. THE PARTY OF KIM IL-SŎNG IN TRANSITION

1. Kim Il-sŏng mentioned these groups in his speech of February 8, 1958. See "The Korean People's Army is the Successor to the anti-Japanese Armed Struggle," Kim Il Sung, *Selected Works*, II, 71–72. For details of the organization and activities of these groups, see my *Politics of Korean Nationalism* (Berkeley, California, 1963).

2. Kim Il Sung, *Selected Works*, I, 200.

3. Ibid., II, 66.

4. Ibid., II, 66–67.

5. Ibid., II, 71–72.

6. Ibid., II, 72–73.

7. See Chapter Six.

8. Their findings were published in a volume entitled *Hang Il mujang t'ujaeng chŏnjŏkji rŭl ch'ajasŏ* (Visiting the Vestigial Remains of the Anti-Japanese Armed Struggle Area), Pyongyang, 1960, 368 pages.

9. For descriptions of the Museum, see Harrison E. Salisbury, *To Peking and Beyond* (New York, 1973), pp. 209–212, and Fred J. Carrier, *North Korean Journey: The Revolution Against Colonialism* (New York, 1975), pp. 96–96.

10. For a study of the Soviet Russian handling of historiography, which is strikingly similar to the situation in North Korea, see Nancy Whittier Heer, *Politics and History in the Soviet Union* (Cambridge, Mass., 1971).

11. Chosŏn Nodong-dang Chungang Wiwŏnhoe chiksok Tang Yŏksa Yŏnguso (Party History Research Center, Central Committee of the Korean Workers' Party), *Hang Il palchisan ch'amgajadŭlŭi hoesanggi* (Recollections of the Participants in the Anti-Japanese Partisan Struggle), Pyongyang, 1959, Tokyo Reprint edition, 1961, pp. 161–163.

12. See Salisbury, *To Peking*, p. 206. It is interesting that an American professor sympathetic to North Korea has written, after a two-week visit there in 1973, that the North Korean practice of enshrining "honored sites" is akin to the American practice of marking sites associated with their founding father. Professor Fred J. Carrier said: "Just as Washington slept in many beds, all duly marked by historical citations, so Kim has sat in many chairs while giving 'on the spot guidance' and these places have become honored sites. The stories of Kim's

deeds are legendary, with one for almost any occasion. Even adults are prone to tell these stories, indicative of how deeply the lessons have been planted." *North Korean Journey*, p. 93.

13. For examples, see Nam Hyo-jae, *Chosŏn ui ŏmŏni* (Mother of Korea), Pyongyang, 1968; Korean Workers' Party, Central Committee, Party History Study Center, *Pulgul ui pan-Il hyŏngmyŏng t'usa Kim Hyŏng-jik sŏnsaeng* (Mister Kim Hyŏng-jik, the Indomitable Anti-Japanese Revolutionary Fighter), Tokyo, 1969; Song Sung-ch'il, *Chosŏn Inmin ui widaehan suryŏng Kim Il-sŏng tongji ui hyŏngmyŏngjŏk kajŏng* (The Revolutionary Family of Comrade Kim Il-sŏng, the Great Leader of the Korean People), Pyongyang, 1969; and Baik Bong, *Kim Il Sung: Biography*, I, 19–39.

14. *Kita Chōsen kenkyū* (Study of North Korea), Tokyo, December 1974, p. 57. Other information concerning Kim Yŏng-ju's career has been drawn from Cho Ch'ŏn-sŏng (ed.), *Ch'ŏllima ui mabu kunsang* (The Drivers of the Flying Horses), Seoul, 1969, p. 127, and Scalapino and Lee, *Communism in Korea*, pp. 608–664.

15. Takigawa Hiroshi, "Kōkeisha Kin Sei-ichi o meguru jōhō" (Information Concerning the Successor Kim Chŏng-il), *Koria Hyōron* (Korea Review), Tokyo, December 1975–January 1976, p. 32.

16. Cited in ibid., pp. 33–35.

17. Ibid., p. 35.

18. Cited in ibid., p. 31.

19. Carrier, *North Korean Journey*, p. 34.

20. The first (and inaugural) congress of the North Korean Workers' Party was held in 1946. The second congress was held in 1948, the third in 1956, the fourth in 1961, and the fifth in 1970.

21. For the rules of the KWP, see Scalapino and Lee, *Communism in Korea*, pp. 1331–1349.

22. The analysis presented here and in the subsequent pages is based on information provided in ibid., Appendix C, "Workers' Party of Korea, Central Committee Members, 1948–1970," pp. 1350–1380.

23. For our previous analysis of the performance of the party and the state in various areas of concern, see ibid., Chapters 8–14.

24. An English translation of the Party Rules of the KWP is available in ibid., pp. 1331–1349. For the "duties of the party member," see article 5 (pp. 1334–1335).

25. "On the Six-Year (1971–1976) Plan for the Development of the National Economy of the Democratic People's Republic," delivered at the November 9, 1970, meeting of the Congress and carried in *Nodong Sinmun* (Labor News, the organ of the KWP), November 6, 1970. See Foreign Broadcast Information Service (FBIS), *Daily Report*, November 10, 1970, as reported by the Korean Central News Agency International Service in English, November 10, 1970. Quoted from Scalapino and Lee, *Communism in Korea*, p. 658.

26. Ibid., pp. 712–713. The figure for 1975, as reported earlier, is from

Carrier, *North Korean Journey*, p. 34.

27. One can also assess the general educational level of the party members by analyzing the occupational categories of the party members. According to Premier Kim Il-sŏng's statement of 1956, the social composition of the 1,164,945 members as of January 1, 1956 was as follows: workers, 22.6 percent; poor farmers, 56.8 percent; "middle farmers," 3.7 percent; office workers, 13.0 percent; and others, 2.9 percent. *Kim Il-sŏng sŏnjip* (Selected Works of Kim Il-sŏng), 1960 ed., IV, 541. One can assume that the first two categories of members, constituting 79.4 percent, were poorly educated.

28. "On the Successful Accomplishment of the Technical Revolution," August 11, 1960, in *Selected Works* (English ed., 1971), II, 553–581.

29. The English text of Kim Il-sŏng's report is available in FBIS *Daily Report*, November 16, 1970, No. 222, Supplement 21.

30. Kim Il-sŏng delivered a major speech on September 24, 1974, "On the Situation of Our Country and Tasks of the League of Korean Youth in Japan," the text of which was published in English in *The People's Korea*, October 16, 1974, pp. 1–3. All references to his speech of March 4, 1975, are based on "Speech of the Great Leader Comrade Kim Il Sung at Meeting of Activists in Industry," Korean Central News Agency dispatch of March 6, as distributed by the Office of the Permanent Observer to the United Nations of the DPRK, March 18, 1975.

31. See note 30 for sources.

32. Chosŏn Minjujuui Inmin Konghwaguk Sahoe Kwahakwŏn Ch'ŏlhak Yŏnguso (Research Center on Philosophy, Academy of Social Science, the Democratic People's Republic of Korea), *Ch'ŏlhak sajŏn* (Dictionary of Philosophy), Pyongyang, 1970, p. 16.

33. A more direct translation of the phrase "through stale formulas" would be "through formula-ism" (tosik-chŏk). "Tosik Chuui" ("graph-ism") from which the adjective "tosik-chŏk" came, means the mechanical attempt to fit new knowledge into predetermined graphs or general formulas.

34. See Scalapino and Lee, *Communism in Korea*, p. 916.

35. Kim Il Sung, *New Year Address*, Pyongyang, 1976, p. 3.

36. In 1966, Kim Il-sŏng announced that there were 170,000 engineers and specialists who were graduates of colleges and 260,000 technicians. The proportion of college graduates in 1966, therefore, was 39.5 percent. Scalapino and Lee, *Communism in Korea*, p. 907. Since it would be more difficult to produce college graduates than others, it is highly probable that less than 40 percent of the one million technical personnel in 1976 are college graduates.

37. Carrier, *North Korean Journey*, p. 33.

38. See the English text as broadcast by the Korean Central News Agency, December 27, 1972, and reported in FBIS *Daily Report*, December 29, 1972, D4–D20.

Bibliography

For materials in Oriental languages—Korean, Japanese, and Chinese—only works cited in the footnotes are listed. This is because rather extensive bibliographies are available elsewhere. For publications before 1972, one should consult Robert A. Scalapino and Chong-Sik Lee, *Communism in Korea* (Berkeley and Los Angeles, University of California Press, 1973), Vol. II, pp. 1426–1491. Publications after that date are listed in Dae-Sook Suh's "Research Materials on North Korea," in Han-Kyo Kim, ed., *Guide to Korean Studies*, scheduled for publication in 1978 by the University of Hawaii Press.

No attempt was made to list materials in the Russian language. Readers are advised to consult George Ginsburgs' *Soviet Works on Korea, 1945–1970* (Los Angeles, University of Southern California Press, 1973), and his chapter on "Russian Language Materials," in Kim's *Guide*.

So far as English-language materials are concerned, an attempt was made to list all noteworthy items published after 1972 by the Foreign Languages Press in Pyongyang, as well as those published outside of North Korea. Pre-1972 publications are listed only if cited in this work. For a more extensive listing of works published before 1972, the reader should consult Scalapino and Lee, *Communism in Korea*, as well as Kim's *Guide*, which, in addition to the two chapters cited above, includes chapters by Joseph Sanghoon Chung on the economy, B. C. Koh on foreign relations and unification policies, and C. I. Eugene Kim on government and politics.

PUBLICATIONS IN ORIENTAL LANGUAGES

Ch'a Rak-hun and Chŏng Kyŏng-mo, eds. *Puk Han pŏpryŏng yŏnhyŏkjip* (North Korean Laws). Seoul, 1969, 779 pp.

Chi, Yun-lung. *Yang Ching-yü ho K'ang Lien Ti-i-lu chün* (Yang Ching-yu and the First Route Army of the Anti-Japanese Allied Army). N.p., 1946, 107 pp.

Cho, Ch'ŏn-sŏng. *Ch'ŏllima ui mabu kunsang* (The Drivers of the Flying Horses). Seoul, 1969, 278 pp. A biographic dictionary.

Chōsen Nōkai (Agricultural Association of Korea). *Chōsen nōgyō hattatsu-shi, Seisaku-hen* (History of Agricultural Development in Korea, Policy Part). Seoul, 1944, 775 pp.

Chōsen Sōtokufu, Hōmu-kyoku (Bureau of Justice, Government-General of Korea). *Chōsen dokuritsu shisō undō no hensen* (Changes in the Korean Independence Thought Movement). Seoul, 1931, 249 pp.

———. Keimukyoku (Police Affairs Bureau, Government-General of Korea). *Saikin ni okeru Chōsen chian jōkyō* (Recent Conditions of Public Security in Korea). Seoul, 1934, 441 pp.

———. Keijō Chihō Hōin, Kenji-kyoku (Prosecutor's Office, Seoul District Court). *Chōsen kyōsantō jiken* (The Korean Communist Party Incident). Seoul, n.d., 40 pp.

Chosŏn Munju Chuui Inmin Konghwaguk, Kwahakwon, Yŏksa Yŏnguso (Center for Historical Studies, Academy of Science, DPRK). *Chosŏn t'ongsa* (An Outline History of Korea). Pyongyang, 1958, 3 vols.

———. Sahoe Kwahakwon Ch'ŏlhak Yŏnguso (Research Center on Philosophy, Academy of Social Science, the DPRK). *Ch'ŏlhak sajŏn* (Dictionary of Philosophy). Pyongyang, 1970, 840 pp.

Chosŏn Nodong-dang Chungang Wiwonhoe chiksok Tang Yŏksa Yŏnguso (Party History Research Center, Central Committee of the Korean Workers' Party). *Hang Il Palchisan ch'amgaja dŭl ŭi hoesanggi* (Recollections of the Participants in the Anti-Japanese Partisan Struggle). Pyongyang, 1959–1961, 8 vols.; 1967 ed., 9 vols.

———. *Pulgul ui pan-Il hyŏngmyŏng t'usa Kim Hyŏng-jik sŏnsaeng* (Mr. Kim Hyŏng-jik, the Indomitable Anti-Japanese Revolutionary Fighter). Tokyo, 1969, 142 pp. Kim Hyŏng-jik is President Kim Il-sŏng's father.

Chosŏn Sanŏp Nodong Chosaso (Research Center for Korean Industry and Labor), eds. *Ol-ŭn nosŏn* (The Correct Line). Seoul, 1945, 30 pp.

Feng, Chung-yün. *Tung-pei K'angjih Lien-chün shih-ssu-nien k'u-tou chien-shih* (Brief History of the Fourteen Years of the Northeastern Anti-Japanese Allied Army). Harbin, 1946, 91 pp.

Han, Hyŏng-gwŏn. "Hyŏngmyŏng-ga ui hoesangrok" (Recollections of a Revolutionary). *Samch'ŏlli*, Seoul, October 1, 1948, pp. 10–11.

Han, Im-hyŏk. *Kim Il-sŏng tongji e ŭihan Chosŏn Kongsandang ch'anggŏn* (The Founding of the Korean Communist Party by Comrade Kim Il-sŏng). Pyongyang, 1961, 56 pp.

Hang-Il mujang t'ujaeng chŏnjŏkchi rŭl ch'ajasŏ (Visiting the Vestigial Remains of the Anti-Japanese Armed Struggle Area). Pyongyang, 1960, 368 pp.

Hu, Ch'iao-mu. *Chungkuo kungch'antang ti sanshih-nien* (Thirty Years of the Chinese Communist Party). Peking, 1952.

Japan, Ministry of Foreign Affairs. "Kōrai kyōsantō oyobi Zenro Kyōsantō no gaikyō" (An Outline of the Koryŏ Communist Party and the All-Russian Communist Party). November 1922, in Archives of the Japanese Ministry of Foreign Affairs; microfilmed for the Library of Congress, Washington, D.C., Reel S721, document S9.4.5.2–30.

Kim, Ch'ang-sun. *Puk-Han sip-o-nyŏn sa* (Fifteen-Year History of North Korea). Seoul, 1961, 283 pp.

Kim, Il-sŏng. *Chayuwa tongnip ŭl wihan Chosŏn inmin ui chŏngui ui choguk haebang chŏnjaeng* (The Korean People's Just Fatherland Liberation War for Freedom and Independence). Pyongyang, 1954, 390 pp. Collection of speeches delivered during the war.

———. *Kim Il-sŏng chŏjak sŏnjip* (Selected Writings of Kim Il-sŏng). Pyongyang, 6 vols., 1967–1973.

———. *Kim Il-sŏng sŏnjip* (Collected Works of Kim Il-sŏng). Pyongyang, 4 vol. ed., 1953–1954; 5 vol. ed., 1960–1964.

———. "Let Us Vigorously Carry Out the Three Revolutions and Further Accelerate Socialist Construction," *Kullŏja* (Worker, Pyongyang), March 1975, pp. 2–22. Stressed, among other things, the need to improve foreign trade.

———. "The Road to Revolution and Construction," *Sekai* (World, Tokyo), February 1976, pp. 186–197. Explains some of the reasons for current economic difficulties.

Kim, Jun-yŏp, *et al.*, eds. *Puk Han yŏngu charyojip* (Materials on North Korean Studies). 2 vols., Seoul, 1969 and 1974. Contains many important documents.

Kim, Jun-yŏp, and Kim Ch'ang-sun. *Hanguk kongsan chu-ŭi undong-sa* (History of the Korean Communist Movement). 4 vols., Seoul, 1969–1975. The most comprehensive and detailed history (1918–1945) of the subject in any language.

Kim, Yak-su. "Killim kwa Namkyong e-sŏ," (In Chilin and Nanking), *Samch'ŏlli*, January 1932, pp. 33–34.

Kim, Yong-gi. *Chosŏn ui nongŏp* (Agriculture in Korea). Seoul, 1946, 115 pp.

Kim, Yun-hwan. *Il-che-ha Hanguk nodong undong ŭi chŏn-gae kwajŏng* (The Developmental Process of the Labor Movement in Korea under Japanese

Imperialism). Ph.D. dissertation, Korea University, 1968, mimeographed. The most detailed work on the subject available in any language.

Kin Nichisei senshū (Selected Works of Kim Il-sŏng). Kyoto, 1952, 3 vols. Contains some materials not included in the various editions of the *Selected Works* published by the Party in Pyongyang.

Manchukuo, Gunseibu, Komonbu (Military Dept., Advisory Section). *Manshū kyōsanhi no kenkyū* (A Study of Communist Insurgents in Manchuria). No place of publication, 1937, 1,069 pp. A detailed study of the anti-Japanese guerrillas in Manchuria.

———. Minseibu, Sōmu-shi, Chōsaka (Research Section, General Affairs Division, Department of Civil Administration). *Zaiman Chōsenjin jijō* (Condition of the Koreans in Manchuria). Changchun, 1933, 222 pp.

Manshūkokushi Hensan Kankōkai (Society to Compile and Publish the History of Manchukuo). *Manshūkokushi* (History of Manchukuo). 2 vols., Tokyo, 1971.

Morita, Yoshio. *Chōsen shūsen no kiroku* (The Record of the End of the War in Korea). Tokyo, 1964, 1038 pp.

Motoi, Tamaki. "How Far Has North Korean Economic Construction Come," *Koria hyōron* (Korea Review, Tokyo), June 1974, pp. 2–15.

Nam, Hyo-jae. *Chosŏn ŭi ŏmŏni* (Mother of Korea). Pyongyang, 1968, 369 pp. Hagiography of President Kim Il-sŏng's mother.

"Preliminary Trial Statement of Kim Ch'an," in Kōtō Hōin, Kenjikyoku (Prosecutor's Office, High Court, Korean Government-General). *Shisō geppō* (Thought Monthly), Vol. 2, No. 2, May 1932, no pagination.

Song, Sŭng-ch'il. *Chosŏn inmin ui widaehan suryŏng Kim Il-sŏng tongji ŭi hyŏngmyŏngjŏk kajŏng* (The Revolutionary Family of Comrade Kim Il-sŏng, the Great Leader of the Korean People). Pyongyang, 1969, 250 pp.

Sun, Chieh. *Tungpei K'ang-Jih Lien-chün ti-ssu-chün* (The Fourth Army of the Northeastern Anti-Japanese Allied Army). Paris (?), 1936, 122 pp.

Suzuki, Kenji. "Kita Chōsen mita mama," (North Korea as I saw it), *Koksai kankei shiryō* (International Relations Materials, Tokyo), Oct. 25, 1975, pp. 1–8.

Takigawa, Hiroshi. "Kōkeisha Kin Sei-ichi o meguru jōhō" (Information Concerning the Successor Kim Chŏng-il), *Koria hyōron* (Korea Review, Tokyo), Dec. 1975–Jan. 1976, pp. 31–37.

Yoshiura, Daizō. *Chōsenjin no kyōsan shugi undō* (Communist Movements of the Koreans). Bureau of Criminal Affairs, Ministry of Justice, Tokyo, 1940, 348 pp.

Yu, Sŏk-in. *Aeguk ŭi pyŏl dŭl* (The Patriotic Stars). Seoul, 1965, 248 pp. Contains the most authoritative biography of Yi Tong-hwi.

Yun, Myŏng-sŏn. "The Miscarriage of Economic Planning in North Korea and the Improvement in Technology," *Koria hyōron* (Korea Review, Tokyo), March 1976, pp. 30–41.

Zenkoku Keizai Chōsa Kikan Rengōkai Chōsen Shibu (Federation of Economic Research Agencies throughout Japan, Korean Branch), ed. *Chōsen keizai nempō* (Korean Economy Annual Report). 1941–1942 ed., Tokyo, 1943.

PUBLICATIONS IN ENGLISH

Appleman, Roy E. *South to Naktong, North to Yalu, June–November, 1950.* Washington, D.C., 1961, 813 pp. Deals extensively with the North Korean forces.

Awanohara, Susumu. "North Korea: Deeper in Debt," *Far Eastern Economic Review*, June 6, 1975.

———. "Pyongyang's Time Runs Out," *Far Eastern Economic Review*, April 9, 1976, pp. 38–39.

Baik Bong. *Kim Il Sung: Biography.* 3 vols., Tokyo, 1969–1970. The latest and most detailed official biography.

Barnds, William J. *The Two Koreas in East Asian Affairs.* New York, 1976, 216 pp. Contains chapters on "North Korea and the Major Powers" (by D. S. Zagoria and Young Kun Kim), and "The Two Koreas—Dialogue or Conflict?" (by R. A. Scalapino).

Borisov, O. B., and B. T. Koloskov. *Soviet-Chinese Relations, 1945–1970,* edited and with an introduction by Vladimir Petrov. Bloomington, Indiana, 1975, 364 pp. Presents information concerning Soviet participation in the Korean War.

Brun, Ellen, and Jacques Hersh. *Socialist Korea: A Case Study in the Strategy of Economic Development.* New York, 1976, 422 pp. A Monthly Review Press publication.

Carrier, Fred J. *North Korean Journey: The Revolution Against Colonialism.* New York, 1975, 120 pp. An American professor sympathetic to the North Korean cause visited North Korea for two weeks in June 1973. Provides some interesting information not available elsewhere.

Cho, Jaekwan. "A Comparative Analysis of the Communist Cadre System," unpublished Ph.D. dissertation, University of California, Berkeley, 1972, 268 pp. Compares the DPRK with China.

Cho, Sung Yoon. "Law and Justice in North Korea," *Journal of Korean Affairs,* January 1973, pp. 3–23.

Chung, Joseph Sang-hoon. *The North Korean Economy: Structure and Development.* Stanford, Ca., 1974, 212 pp. The only monograph on the North Korean economy available in English. Highly competent and reliable.

———. "North Korea's Economic System and the New Constitution," *Journal of Korean Affairs,* April 1973, pp. 28–34.

———. "North Korea's Seven-Year Plan (1961–70), *Asian Survey,* June 1972, pp. 527–45.

———. "Recent Trends in the North Korean State Budget: With Special Reference to 1971 and 1972," *Journal of Korean Affairs,* January 1973, pp. 24–30.

"Claiming Success in North Korea," *Far Eastern Economic Review,* January 31, 1975, pp. 50–55.

Clemens, Walter C., Jr. "GRIT at Panmunjom: Conflict and Cooperation in a Divided Korea," *Asian Survey,* June 1973, pp. 531–559. "GRIT" stands for "graduated reciprocation in tension reduction."

Communist International. *From the Fourth to the Fifth World Congress: Report of the Executive Committee of the Communist International.* London, 1924, 122 pp.

Comrade Kim Il Sung, An Ingenious Thinker and Theoretician. Pyongyang, 1975, 160 pp. Compendium of essays by foreigners.

Cumings, Bruce G. "Kim's Korean Communism," *Problems of Communism,* March–April 1974, pp. 27–40.

Democratic People's Republic of Korea, Academy of Sciences, Research Institute of History. *History of the Just Fatherland Liberation War of the Korean People.* Pyongyang, 1961, 323 pp.

Djilas, Milovan. *Conversations with Stalin.* New York, 1962, 211 pp.

Eudin, Xenia Joukoff, and Robert C. North, eds. *Soviet Russia and the East, 1920–1927: A Documentary Survey.* Stanford, Ca., 1957, 478 pp.

Fulkerson, Frank B. "The Mineral Industry of North Korea," in U.S. Dept. of Interior, *Bureau of Mines Minerals Yearbook,* 1973, reprint 7 pp.

Gayn, Mark. "The Cult of Kim," *New York Times Magazine,* October 1, 1972, pp. 16–34. A veteran journalist's account of his visit to North Korea.

Ginsburgs, George. *Soviet Works on Korea, 1945–1970.* Los Angeles, 1973, 279 pp. An essay and a 1,126-item bibliography on wide-ranging subjects.

Ginsburgs, George, and Roy U. T. Kim. *Calendar of Diplomatic Affairs: Democratic People's Republic of Korea, 1945–1975.* Moorestown, N.J., 1977, 250 pp.

Grajdanzev, Andrew J. *Modern Korea.* New York, 1944, 330 pp.

Heer, Nancy Whittier. *Politics and History in the Soviet Union.* Cambridge, 1971, 319 pp.

Historical Experience of Agricultural Cooperation in Our Country. Pyongyang, 1975, 171 pp. Sets forth the KWP's position on agricultural cooperatives.

Hsiao, Kung-chuan. *Rural China: Imperial Control in the Nineteenth Century.* Seattle, 1960, 783 pp.

Jo, Yung-Hwan. "Whither Two Koreas?" *Pacific Community*, July 1974, pp. 565–78.

Jones, P. H. M. "Economic Survey of North Korea," *The Far East and Australasia.* London, 1974, pp. 873–877.

Juhn, Daniel Sungil. "The North Korean Managerial System at the Factory Level," *Journal of Korean Affairs,* April 1972, pp. 16–21.

Kang, Young Hoon. "Kim Il Sung's Trip to Peking," *Journal of Korean Affairs,* April 1975, pp. 47–52.

———. "The Military-Security Implications of the North-South Korean Dialogue," *Journal of Korean Affairs,* July 1974, pp. 1–7.

Khruschev, Nikita. *Khrushchev Remembers.* Boston, 1970, 639 pp. Introduction and notes by Edward Crankshaw; translated and edited by Strobe Talbott.

Kim Chin. "Law of Marriage and Divorce in North Korea," *International Lawyer,* 1973 (no. 4), pp. 906–17.

———. "North Korean Nationality Law," *International Lawyer,* 1972 (no. 2), pp. 324–29.

Kim, H. Edward. "Rare Look at North Korea," *National Geographic,* August 1974, pp. 252–77. Rare photographs and an essay by a Korean-American of keen perception and sensitivity, who visited North Korea for 20 days in October 1973.

Kim, Han-kyo, ed. *Reunification of Korea: 50 Basic Documents.* Washington, D.C., 1972, 83 pp. Includes a number of statements issued by North Korean leaders and organizations.

Kim, Ilpyong J. *Communist Politics in North Korea.* New York, 1975, 121 pp. Presents topical analysis of North Korea's leadership, ideology, techniques of mass mobilization, and foreign relations. Eschews criticism and strongly reflects North Korea's official views.

———. "North Korea: Economic Development," *Problems of Communism,* January–February 1973, pp. 44–54.

Kim, Il Sung. "All Efforts to Attain the Goal of Eight Million Tons of Grain," *Pyongyang Times,* January 25, 1975. A speech delivered at the National Congress of Agriculture.

———. *For the Independent Peaceful Reunification of Korea.* New York, 1975, 230 pp. Compendium of Kim's speeches delivered between 1948 and 1974. Revised edition, 1976, 246 pp., includes speeches delivered between 1975 and 1976.

———. *Juche! The Speeches and Writing of Kim Il Sung,* edited and introduced by Li Yuk-Sa. New York, 1972, 271 pp. Foreword by Eldridge Cleaver. Selected works of the 1964–1970 period.

———. *New Year Address.* Pyongyang, 1976, 9 pp.

———. *On Juche in Our Revolution.* Pyongyang, 1975, 2 vols. Compendium of Kim's speeches emphasizing the nationalist theme between 1931 and 1974. Speeches allegedly delivered before 1945 and are presumably reconstructed from memory.

———. *On the Occasion of the 30th Anniversary of the Foundation of the Workers' Party of Korea.* Pyongyang, 1975, 49 pp. One of the major speeches.

———. "On the Situation of Our Country and Tasks of the League of Korean Youth in Japan," *The People's Korea* (Pyongyang), Oct. 16, 1974, pp. 1–3. One of Kim's major speeches in 1974.

———. *Selected Works.* Pyongyang, 1971, 4 vols; 1975–76, 6 vols.

———. *Talk with the Editor-in-chief of the Japanese Politico-Theoretical Magazine "Sekai,"* Pyongyang, 1976, 29 pp. Presents the views of the DPRK as of March 1976.

———. *The Youth Must Take over the Revolution and Carry it Forward.* Pyongyang, 1976, 245 pp. Compendium of addresses delivered before youth groups in North Korea, 1946–1971.

Kim, Joungwon A. *Divided Korea: The Politics of Development, 1945–1972.* Cambridge, Mass.: Harvard University Press, 1975, 471 pp. Devotes three chapters to North Korea. Occasionally presents fresh insights. Very useful.

Kim, Kwang. "Approaches to the Problem of Korean Unification: A Study in Linkage Politics," unpublished Ph.D. dissertation, New York University, 1974, 391 pp. Includes a discussion of North Korean policy and strategy toward the South.

Kim, Yong Soon. "Politics of Korean Unification: A Comparative Study of Systemic Outputs in Two Different Political Systems," unpublished Ph.D. dissertation, Rutgers University 1974, 115 pp.

Kim, Young C. ed. *Foreign Policies of Korea.* Washington, D.C., 1973, 128 pp. Contains three papers on North Korea's foreign relations, including a paper on foreign trade.

———, ed. *Major Powers and Korea.* Silver Spring, Maryland, 1973, 164 pp. Compendium of papers delivered at a conference sponsored by the Research Institute on Korean Affairs.

———. "North Korea in 1974," *Asian Survey,* January 1975, pp. 43–52.

———. "North Korea's Reunification Policy: A Magnificent Obsession?" *Journal of Korean Affairs,* January 1974, pp. 15–24. An account of talks with North Korean cadres during the author's short visit to North Korea in the previous year.

Kloth, Edward W. "The Korean Path to Socialism: The Taean Industrial Management System" *Occasional Papers on Korea,* No. 3 (June 1975), pp. 34–48.

Koh, B. C. "Chuch'esong in Korean Politics," *Studies in Comparative Communism,* Spring–Summer 1974, pp. 83–106.

———. "The Korean Workers' Party and Détente," *Journal of International Affairs,* 1974 (No. 2), pp. 187–95.

———. "North Korea: A Breakthrough in the Quest for Unity," *Asian Survey,* January 1973, pp. 83–93.

———. "North Korea: Old Goals and New Realities," *Asian Survey,* January 1974, pp. 36–42.

———. "South Korea, North Korea and Japan," *Pacific Community,* January 1975, pp. 205–219.

———. "The United Nations and the Politics of Korean Reunification," *Journal of Korean Affairs,* January 1974, pp. 37–56.

Korean Information Service. *North Korea: Seen from Abroad.* Seoul, 1976, 153 pp. Reprints of critical newspaper articles on North Korean economy and politics published abroad between June 1974 and May 1976.

Korean Review. Pyongyang, 1974, 183 pp. An official handbook on North Korean society, politics, and economy.

Koyosaki, Wayne S. *North Korea's Foreign Relations: The Politics of Accommodation, 1945–75.* New York, 1976, 133 pp. A brisk and informative analysis of North Korea's relationship with the Soviet Union and China.

Lee, Changsoo. "Chosoren: An Analysis of the Korean Communist Movement in Japan," *Journal of Korean Affairs,* July 1973, pp. 3–32.

Lee, Chong-Sik. "The Détente and Korea," in William E. Griffith, ed., *The World and the Great-Power Triangles.* Cambridge, Mass., 1975, pp. 321–96, 446–53.

———. "The Impact of the Sino-American Détente on Korea," in Gene T. Hsiao, ed., *Sino-American Détente and its Policy Implications.* New York, 1974, pp. 189–206.

———, ed., *Materials on Korean Communism, 1945–1947,* Honolulu, Hawaii, 1977, 254 pp.

———. "The 1972 Constitution and Top Communist Leaders," in Dae-Sook Suh and Chae-Jin Lee, eds., *Political Leadership in Korea.* Seattle, Washington, 1976, pp. 192–219.

———. "New Paths for North Korea," *Problems of Communism,* March–April 1977, pp. 55–66.

———. *The Politics of Korean Nationalism.* Berkeley, Ca., 1963, 342 pp.

———. "Stalinism, in the East: Communism in North Korea," in Robert A. Scalapino, ed., *The Communist Revolution in Asia.* Englewood Cliffs, N.J., 1965, pp. 114–39. Revised ed., 1969, pp. 120–50.

———. "Witch Hunt Among the Guerrillas: The Min-sheng-t'uan Incident," *China Quarterly,* April–June 1966, pp. 107–17.

——— and Ki-Wan Oh. "The Russian Faction in North Korea," *Asian Survey,* April 1968, pp. 270–88.

Lee, Joung-Koon. "North Korean Foreign Trade in Recent Years and the Prospects for North-South Korean Trade," *Journal of Korean Affairs,* October 1974, pp. 18–32.

Lee, Mun Woong. *Rural North Korea Under Communism: A Study of Sociocultural Change.* Houston, Rice University Studies, vol. 62, no. 1, 1976, 176 pp. Revision of a Ph.D. dissertation. Contains a useful bibliography.

Lee, Pong S. "An Estimate of North Korea's National Income," *Asian Survey,* June 1972, pp. 518–26.

———. "North Korean Economy in the Seventies: A Survey," *Journal of Korean Affairs,* October 1974, pp. 3–17.

Lewis, John Wilson. *Leadership in Communist China.* Ithaca, New York, 1963, 305 pp.

———, ed., *Party Leadership and Revolutionary Power in China.* New York, 1970, 422 pp.

Mao Tse-tung. *Selected Works of Mao Tse-tung.* New York, 4 vols., 1954–1956.

Moore, Stanley. "North Korea Identifying the Peninsula Threat," *Far Eastern Economic Review,* January 22, 1973, pp. 16–18.

Nam, Koon Woo. *The North Korean Communist Leadership, 1945–1965,* University, Alabama, 1974, 214 pp. A study of the factional struggles in North Korea leading to the victory of Kim Il-sŏng.

On the Question of Korea: Speeches of Representatives at the 29th Session of the U.N. General Assembly. Pyongyang, 1975, 238 pp. Speeches by delegates from various nations that supported the North Korean position.

On the Socialist Constitution of the Democratic People's Republic of Korea. Pyongyang, 1975, 329 pp. Contains President Kim Il-sŏng's speech delivered on December 25, 1972, to introduce the new constitution, the text and explanations of the provisions of the constitution, and principal laws adopted by the DPRK since 1948.

Paige, Glenn D. *The Korean Decision, June 24–30, 1950.* New York, 1968, 394 pp.

Rhee, Sang-Woo. "Themes of North Korea's Unification Messages: A Study on Pattern Shifts, 1948–1968," *Korean Journal of International Studies,* Spring 1973, pp. 7–36. Content analysis of North Korean messages pertaining to unification.

Salisbury, Harrison E. *To Peking and Beyond: A Report on the New Asia.* New York,

1973, 308 pp. Devotes two chapters to his travels in North Korea, where he spent two weeks in May 1972.

Scalapino, Robert A. "China and the North-South (Korea) Negotiations," *Korean Journal of International Studies,* October, 1973, pp. 73–86.

———. *The Japanese Communist Movement, 1920–1966,* Berkeley, California, 1967, 412 pp.

——— and Chong-Sik Lee. *Communism in Korea,* 2 vols., Berkeley, California, 1973.

——— and Chong-Sik Lee. "The Origins of the Korean Communist Movement, *Journal of Asian Studies,* XX (1) and (2), November 1960 and February 1961, pp. 9–31, 149–67.

Shinn, Rinn-sup. "Changing Perspectives in North Korea: Foreign and Reunification Policies," *Problems of Communism,* January–February 1973, pp. 55–71.

Simmons, Robert R. "North Korea: Year of the Thaw," *Asian Survey,* January 1972, pp. 25–31.

———. *The Strained Alliance: Peking, Pyongyang, Moscow, and the Politics of the Korean Civil War.* New York, 1975, 287 pp. Challenges some of the conclusions reached by earlier studies on the origins of the Korean War.

Smith, Gaddis. "After 25 Years—The Parallel," *New York Times Magazine,* June 22, 1975, pp. 15–25.

Soh, Jin Chull. "The Role of the Soviet Union in Preparation of the Korean War," *Journal of Korean Affairs,* January 1974, pp. 3–14.

Song, Byung Soon. "Comparative Study of Ideological Influences on Educational Theory and Practice in North and South Korea," unpublished Ph.D. dissertation, Wayne State University, 1974.

Spahr, William. "The Military Security Aspects of Soviet Relations with North Korea," *Journal of Korean Affairs,* April 1974, pp. 1–8.

Stelmach, Daniel S. "The Influence of Russian Armored Tactics on the North Korean Invasion of 1950," unpublished Ph.D. dissertation, St. Louis University, 1973, 348 pp.

Suh, Dae-Sook. "Communist Party Leadership," in Dae-Sook Suh and Chae-Jin Lee, eds., *Political Leadership in Korea.* Seattle, Washington, 1976, pp. 159–91.

———, ed. *Documents of Korean Communism,. 1918–1948.* Princeton, 1970, 570 pp.

———. *The Korean Communist Movement, 1918–1948,* Princeton, N.J., 1967, 406 pp.

Suhrke, Astri. "Gratuity or Tyranny: The Korean Alliances," *World Politics,*

July 1973, pp. 508–32. Includes discussion of North Korea's relations with the Soviet Union.

White, D. Gordon. "The Democratic People's Republic of Korea Through the Eyes of a Visiting Sinologist," *China Quarterly,* September 1975, pp. 515–22. The author visited North Korea for two weeks in April and May of 1974.

———. "North Korean Chuch'e: The Political Economy of Independence," *Bulletin of Concerned Asian Scholars,* April-June 1975, pp. 44–50.

Whiting, Allan. *Soviet Policies in China, 1917–1924.* New York, 1953, 350 pp.

Yoo, Se Hee. "The Communist Movement and the Peasants: The Case of Korea," in John Wilson Lewis, ed., *Peasant Rebellion and Communist Revolution in Asia,* Stanford, Ca., 1974, pp. 61–76.

———. "The Korean Communist Movement and the Peasantry under Japanese Rule," unpublished Ph.D. dissertation, Columbia University, 1974, 353 pp.

Zagoria, Donald S., and Young Kun Kim. "North Korea and the Major Powers," *Asian Survey,* December 1975, pp. 1017–35. The same article appeared as a chapter in Barnds, ed., *The Two Koreas in East Asian Affairs.*

Index